it happened to me

A Teen's Guide to Overcoming Sexual Abuse

Wm. Lee Carter, Ed.D.

New Harbinger Publications, Inc.

Publisher's Note

This publication is designed to provide accurate and authoritative information in regard to the subject matter covered. It is sold with the understanding that the publisher is not engaged in rendering psychological, financial, legal, or other professional services. If expert assistance or counseling is needed, the services of a competent professional should be sought.

Distributed in the U.S.A. by Publishers Group West; in Canada by Raincoast Books; in Great Britain by Airlift Book Company, Ltd.; in South Africa by Real Books, Ltd.; in Australia by Boobook; and in New Zealand by Tandem Press.

Copyright © 2002 by Wm. Lee Carter
New Harbinger Publications, Inc.
5674 Shattuck Avenue
Oakland, CA 94609

Cover design by Salmon Studios
Cover images by Photodisc/Getty Images (models only, used for illustrative purposes)
Edited by Heather Mitchener
Book design by Michele Waters

ISBN 1-57224-279-5 Paperback

New Harbinger Publications' Web site address: www.newharbinger.com

04   03   02

10   9   8   7   6   5   4   3   2   1

First printing

Contents

Relating to Others   113

Getting Better   149

Let's Get Started

Mention the word "sex" and most teens blush . . . or giggle . . . or smile . . . or feel butterflies . . . or cringe . . . or turn away their eyes . . . or feel sick to their stomach. Can all these different reactions really be true? Yes, because a teenager's thoughts and feelings about sex are perhaps the most personal she experiences. And rightly so, for a teenager's sexuality strikes at the heart of who she is, how she relates, and how she gets along in the world. What *you* feel about the word "sex" is closely connected to your personal experiences with others.

If the topic of sex is personal for all young people, then the matter of sexual abuse is doubly so. Most survivors of sexual trauma have heard statistics telling how widespread sexual abuse is among children, teenagers, and young adults. Maybe it helps a survivor to know that she is not alone in her troubles. Maybe not. The fact that literally millions of young people have been violated in this most personal way is not especially comforting. Despite that, recovery is made easier (if recovery can *ever* be called "easy") when one teenager knows that others share her condition. Most every survivor goes through emotions that include:

- Loneliness

- Shame

- Guilt

- Confusion

- Fear

- Depression

The experience of sexual abuse is an intensely personal matter. Some teenagers feel crippled because of their experience—emotionally, socially, spiritually, and personally. Some find that they have an amazing supply of strength—guts—which helps them make it through their ordeal. Others don't know how to cope and don't know where to begin.

Wherever you are at this stage in your life, you have no doubt figured out one thing: *The experience of sexual abuse demands a response from you.* Try as you may, you cannot ignore it. You have choices to make. You can . . .

Let your past defeat you

Resist the emotional struggle inside you

Get stuck in a cycle of self-defeating thoughts and behaviors

Or:

Explore your heart, soul, and mind to learn from your experiences

Refuse to allow people who have hurt you to control your present and future

Reshape your self-concept and become what you are capable of being

Some Basics

As you take yourself through this workbook, you will be asked to reflect upon different ways that you have been affected by your life experiences. You can do it. You'll be a stronger person for it. It will help you to know some of my beliefs as you read the following pages. They include the following thoughts:

★ No matter where you are at this stage in life, no matter what mistakes you have made, no matter how many bridges you have burned, *you are capable of moving forward in life.* Right now you may be overwhelmed by negative emotions—bitterness, self-destruction, anger, and so on. Those emotions are a natural result of the frustrations you feel because your most basic needs for love, acceptance, security, and self-esteem have been violated. But whatever negative emotions you feel right now do not define you. By nature you have positive tendencies. Recovery is a journey that takes you back to goodness.

★ Recovery from any injury requires hard work. For example, if you broke a leg or had surgery, you would have to rehabilitate before being fully restored to health. Recovery from emotional trauma requires the same hard work. A mistake that many sexual abuse victims make is to believe that as time passes, the effect of that abuse will fade away. True, time contributes to the healing process, but in the long run, therapeutic healing demands work. (And successful survivors all agree that the effort they put into their recovery is worth the results.)

★ The greatest form of evaluation is *self-evaluation.* What others think of you should not be the light that guides you into the future. Your belief about yourself is ultimately the most important ingredient in creating lasting change. Sure, it's wise to accept feedback from people who love you and friends you can trust. The support, belief, and encouragement of others go a long way in helping you get where you want to be. In the end, though, *you* must decide if you are being true to yourself and if you are being honest with others.

★ *Love* and *grace* are perhaps two of the most important experiences in a trauma survivor's recovery. The most basic of all human needs is the need to be loved by others and by one's self. Love is a peculiar emotion. Before you can give it away, you must fill up your own emotional tank. The experience of sexual abuse can leave a victim feeling both unloved and unlovable. Feeling empty, the victim may have difficulty loving others. Grace is an emotion that helps you grow. You experience grace when you meet someone who does not judge or evaluate you. You experience grace when you let yourself receive the warmth, interest, and respect of others. But in an intensely personal way, you experience grace when you learn to love yourself. In a wonderfully circular process, teenagers who love themselves can truly love others. And the experience of love allows that remarkable sense of grace—that feeling that life is good in spite of its hardships—to flood your personality. Together, love and grace allow you to receive and give all the best that people can offer.

Personal Thoughts

When people ask me about the teenage sexual abuse survivors I see in my private practice, one question surfaces more frequently than others. "Did that *really* happen to them?" People also regularly ask, "How do teenagers ever get over being sexually abused?"

Abuse happens. Victims are hurt. It's just not fair that so many innocent children and teenagers are so horribly mistreated. But . . . many survive. Not only can abuse victims survive, they can thrive. I believe that within every human soul is a desire to be better, to move forward, to be healthy. Call it survival instinct, or God-given value, or guts. Whatever it is, teenagers who have been abused *want* to beat their problem.

Most of what you will read and experience in this workbook has been presented to the marvelous teenagers in my practice. My office is on the campus of a psychiatric hospital and residential treatment center in central Texas dedicated to children and teenagers. All the young people who receive treatment from the caring staff at our center have emotional problems of one variety or another. Most have been sexually abused. While each resident is treated with personal attention and concern, sexual abuse victims share common characteristics. Most all of them . . .

- Need—even want—to talk about their experience, no matter how painful

- Question who they are and where life will take them

- Experience confused, often disfigured emotions

- Aren't quite sure how to relate to others

- Want to get better

You will hear from some of the wonderful teenagers I work with. Scattered throughout this workbook are "Voices of Victory" spoken by real-life teens, young people just like you. I suspect that you who are reading this workbook are right where they have been. My sincere hope is that you will get to where many of them have gone. It's not an easy road. Recovery from sexual abuse is hard work. You may want to give up. You may think you can't do it.

Listen to the voices of victory.

Those who have taken themselves through the rigorous paces of trauma recovery will tell you that once they break through the pain barrier and look back on their experiences, their hard work was worth the effort. The teenagers who taste success in recovery have several things in common. They . . .

- ◇ Take advantage of the support of friends, caring adults, and family

- ◇ Want to learn, and soak up every chance to figure out something new about themselves and others

- ◇ Learn from people who have been down the road before them

- ◇ Give to those who come along behind them

- ◇ Learn not to fight their troublesome feelings, but to use them

- ◇ Look for a community to join

Through the years I have learned many things from teenagers. One lesson stands out: *Teenagers are in a prime time of life. They are at an age when they can change. That age will not last long. While adults can change, too, it is the teenage years that are the best time to make permanent life adjustments.*

Listen to the voices of victory.

How This Workbook Can Help You

Sexual abuse affects a victim in more ways than one. Recovery from abuse requires exploration of the many areas affected by that trauma. This workbook attempts to address a wide range of issues that you will face as you move ahead in life. Because of your abuse, many things have changed for you: your emotions, behaviors, social and family relationships, self-concept (what you think of yourself), and personal belief system. You will be taken through reflective exercises intended to . . .

1. Inform you about different aspects of trauma recovery

2. Connect you to the thoughts and emotions of others who have been right where you are now

3. Provoke you to pull together your own ideas and beliefs about yourself and others

4. Allow you to express yourself in an honest and healing manner

5. Help you collect your thoughts so that you can share yourself with others

6. Empower you to confidently become stronger and healthier

7. Nudge you toward new ways of thinking, feeling, and relating

8. Encourage you to love yourself and allow you to give love to others

Not every written activity will directly relate to your experience of abuse. While it's important to tell your story and make sense of what happened, it's equally important to pick up the fragments of the damage that has been done to your emotions, behavior, self-concept, and social interactions and put together the pieces of the puzzle that make your life unique. Recovery *can* happen, and this workbook intends to help you in that effort.

Getting Down to Business

Before beginning the work that follows, review the following guidelines to make sure you are doing all you can to overcome your experience of sexual trauma:

1. If you are currently being abused and no one knows about your situation, tell a person who can help. A trusted adult friend, teacher, responsible family member, law enforcement official, or social agency worker can help you get started in your recovery. Don't fool yourself into believing that the abuse will end on its own. It might not. Be courageous enough to admit your need for help, even if your plea for help ruffles someone else's feathers. Recovery requires that you be properly selfish.

2. Do not attempt to deal with personal matters unless you are truly ready to confront tough and sometimes unpleasant thoughts and feelings. One of the best experiences you can ever have is the feeling that comes when you know you have shucked a heavy burden that once hung around your neck. But one of life's worst experiences can be to tackle tough issues if you are not ready and willing to work at personal growth. Opening yourself to personal exploration carries a responsibility to work hard. Set yourself up for success, not failure.

3. Check yourself and your current relationships. If you are still linked to people who are hurting you, make the decision to move on to relationships that help you. You are a better person than to stay stuck in a cycle of defeat. Trying to overcome the effect of sexual abuse while in the midst of any type of ongoing abuse is comparable to taking swimming lessons in water that is over your head. You have to fight so hard to stay afloat that you can't learn what you want to learn.

4. Don't hesitate to seek professional help as you make your way to personal wholeness. Professionals who specialize in the treatment of sexual trauma can be of immense value as you try to make sense of your thoughts and feelings. Make sure you feel personally comfortable with the counselor or psychologist you talk to. The personal connection between you and a therapist makes all the difference in the work you accomplish.

5. Some readers may wish to go through this workbook alone, keeping their reflections private. Others may want to share their reflections with a friend or counselor or with others who are also completing the workbook. Decide how you wish to make use of the written exercises and use them in a way that benefits you most. You are in control of what you think and how you share yourself with others.

6. Use this workbook as a stepping-stone for further personal growth. One of the most exciting truths about life is that none of us ever reaches the point where we know everything there is to know. The discoveries you make and conclusions you draw over the next few days, weeks, and months will prepare you for further discoveries as you grow older. Rather than use this workbook to find all the answers to your current questions, use it to help you find answers that lead you to newer and deeper questions. By looking at personal growth as an endless process, you will find that life never grows dull—there's always the promise that new discoveries lie beyond the point where you currently stand.

Who Should Use This Workbook

This workbook is designed for a variety of uses. The primary audience is those teenagers who have experienced sexual abuse at any time in their life and are at a point of wanting to learn from their experience so that they may become stronger in spite of (or even because of) it. Since the incidence of sexual trauma is more common among females than males, the language used generally reflects a feminine point of view. Most trauma survivors find that it is in the teenage and early adult years that they have the right combination of desire, thinking skills, insight, and support to begin the process of healing. There is something about youth that makes recovery seem possible. It is those survivors who were kept in mind as this workbook was written.

This workbook can be used by individuals for it allows the reader to move at her own pace through the reflective exercises. Though topics are grouped by categories, an individual may find herself attracted to some portions of the workbook more than others. For a well-rounded approach to recovery, the reader is encouraged to work through all written exercises.

This workbook can be used by groups for it lends itself to discussions among individuals brought together by their shared past. Those readers who find themselves in a group setting are encouraged to express themselves openly and honestly as reflections are shared. The mutual exercise of giving and receiving support is healing in itself. To know that you are not alone in your struggles gives you strength to push on because someone has already blazed a trail ahead of you.

This workbook can be used in individual counseling because the survivor can bring to therapy sessions a written account of the thoughts and questions she would like to discuss on a personal level. Therapists find it helpful to know the intimate concerns young people are dealing with and can assist in clearing up the questions raised while working the reflective exercises. In turn, clients can broach subjects in need of further exploration by sharing workbook entries with the therapist.

Workbook Format

Healing is incomplete if a survivor is spoon-fed answers about personal problems. That's why each chapter of this book is intended to give you an overview of multiple therapeutic topics and prompt you to discover what *you* think about the issues being addressed. Throughout each chapter are scattered probing questions and opportunities to write what you think and feel. These exercises are meant to spur you to put your thoughts, feelings, and opinions into your own words. Teenagers find that as time passes, their musings change. That's exactly as healing should be. Once change begins, the young person cannot stand still but moves from one point in her life to another. It's okay if you reread your written responses days or weeks after writing them and find that you've made new personal discoveries. In fact, that's great!

Also scattered throughout the workbook are quotes from teenagers I know who have moved beyond the pain of sexual trauma. You will find other thoughts and information intended to make you think about your current situation. As you wend your way through this workbook, remain open at all times to your experience. Your ability to listen to yourself marks the beginning of self-acceptance and personal healing.

Grace to you.

Your Experience

Your Feelings—What Do They Mean?

When you were abused, you probably reacted in many different ways. Some of the reactions were physical. Others were emotional. Some reactions occurred at the time of your abuse. Other reactions came later. Common emotional reactions to abuse include the following:

⋄ Confusion

⋄ Shock

⋄ Guilt

⋄ Paranoia

⋄ Disgust

⋄ Denial

⋄ Anger

⋄ Shame

⋄ Nausea

⋄ Numbness

⋄ Betrayal

⋄ Fear

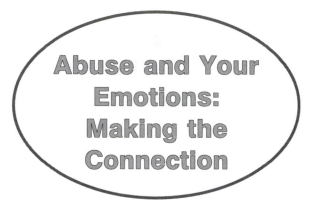

Abuse and Your Emotions: Making the Connection

Of course, other emotional reactions could be added to the above list. Here's something you might not have known:

Every emotional reaction to an event (in this case abuse) has a purpose.

Perhaps you've been told that you are depressed, or mentally ill, or emotionally disturbed because your emotions are out of whack. And maybe they *are* out of whack! But when you stop to think about why you felt the way you did when you were abused, your emotions suddenly begin to make sense.

It's one thing to identify your feelings, but another thing altogether to understand them. It can be tempting to ignore the message of your emotions. To recall how you felt when you were abused may bring back unwanted memories. But young people who understand their emotions have real power—power to control themselves and influence others!

Too often, abuse victims focus on their emotions but ignore the positive message that lies beneath. A part of healing involves listening to yourself. When you reacted to abuse with a particular emotion, your body and mind were communicating something very important. Maybe you did not understand yourself at the time. Others probably failed to understand you, too.

It's not wrong to feel what you feel. Your emotional symptoms are simply a reaction to what happened to you. But you can learn to use your emotions in a way that helps you grow.

Your Reflections

Think back on a time when you were abused and try to remember how you felt. Can you name the emotions you experienced *at the time*? (It's okay to name several emotions.)

_____

_____

_____

_____

Are there other emotions you felt a few days, weeks, months, or even years later?

_____

_____

_____

For each emotion you felt, ask yourself these questions:

Where did the emotion come from? Why did I feel that way?

_____

_____

_____

Is it hard to give myself permission to feel the way I did? Explain.

_____

_____

_____

What is a positive thing I learned from this emotional reaction?

_____

_____

_____

How might this emotional reaction hurt me if I use it the wrong way?

_____

_____

_____

Something I have discovered about myself is:

_____

_____

Think About It!

Your understanding of emotions changes as you change. A small child cannot comprehend the things a teenager can comprehend. A teenager cannot comprehend what a middle-aged adult can comprehend, who in turn cannot comprehend what an elderly adult can comprehend. Rather than get stuck viewing an emotion one particular way, know that as time passes you can find new meaning in the feelings you experience. Your emotions are a gift intended to protect rather than harm you.

Voices of Victory

Everybody told me that I would feel better after time passed. That didn't happen with me. I got worse. Then I figured out why. I got worse because I was sitting around just waiting for time to go by. I wasn't doing anything about my abuse. Once I started to work on my issues, I got better.

—*Annie, age 16*

Useful Tip

If you are experiencing emotional pain, that's not all bad. Really! Just like a fever actually helps your body eventually feel better, an emotional "fever" can push you to get the help you want and deserve. Emotional pain is not something you must put up with forever. You can defeat it. Use your emotional discomfort as a motivator to change. Decide to work hard at improving your situation and, in time, change will happen.

Family Messages

Most teenagers don't realize it, but they soak up messages about themselves from the way family members treat them—especially mothers, fathers, and other adult caregivers. By the time children become teens and young adults, they know exactly how family members think. Think of how many times you have started a sentence that begins something like this:

"My mother/father always says . . ."

"When I was young, we used to . . ."

"My father/mother told me at least a hundred times that I am . . ."

"The way my family does it is . . ."

Before you could talk, you began to think of yourself as good or bad, pretty or ugly, valuable or useless. In time, you developed an image of yourself, a *self-image*. Some of your beliefs were based on general messages you received from adults in your home. They may not have been directly about you, but these messages helped shape the way you think about yourself. For example:

"I'm in charge around here. You're supposed to do what I say."

"Girls (or boys) aren't allowed to act like that in this family."

"Those teachers of yours are always sticking their nose where it doesn't belong."

"Black (or white or yellow) people are just that way."

The general opinions and behaviors modeled by the adults around you played a large role in how you view your world—and how you view yourself. In addition, many specific remarks and gestures were aimed directly at you. Your self-image was shaped in large part by these messages, too. For example, you may have been told:

"If you tell your mother what happened, she'll think you're a whore."

"Keep acting like that and no one will ever trust you."

"I've known kids half your age who can do better than you."

"It's your fault that things in this home are like they are."

Family messages have a huge impact on the way your define yourself. Sometimes, that influence is good. At other times it's not. Too often, adults try to control how kids define themselves. Now that you are able to think like an adult, you can evaluate your family's messages. You may decide to keep some of them. Others you will want to throw away. As you go through this examination process, you are defining yourself, perhaps even *redefining* yourself. A young person's self-image should never remain the same. Just as your body changes and grows, your "self" constantly unfolds. You are a work in progress!

Sound Off

What were some of the *general* messages (opinions, beliefs, expectations) you heard from your family?

_____

_____

_____

What were some of the *specific* family messages aimed directly at you?

_____

_____

_____

Did the men in your family give a different set of messages than the women? If so, what was the difference in the beliefs of the men and women of your family?

_____

_____

_____

_____

How does your family treat boys and girls *differently*?

_____

_____

_____

_____

Finish these sentences . . .

Messages I received from my family that I should keep are:

1.

2.

3.

Messages I received from my family that I should throw away are:

1.

2.

3.

What should I think about myself???

Think About It! The past is permanent, but you can make your own present. Teenagers who say, "If only . . ." or "I wish I had . . ." or "I regret . . ." tend to stick with family messages that drag them down rather than build them up. Replacing those statements with "I'm going to . . ." or "I will . . ." or "I believe . . ." puts you in control of yourself.

Useful Tip

You can take steps to keep family problems from dragging you down to a level of unhappiness or despair.

- Name the things about your family that bother you. If it helps, write them down.

- Describe the ways that you react to family problems. Do you fight back? Rebel? Withdraw? From now on, try to avoid reactions that only make family problems worse.

- If it's possible to share your thoughts and feelings with your family, respectfully do so. If sharing your thoughts and feelings only makes them worse, share them with a counselor or friend. Make sure that you are not simply complaining. Use these talks to figure things out.

- Do what's right even if family members do not.

- If it's necessary, emotionally separate from family members. Learn to look at their behavior as their problem, not yours.

Uncovering Emotional Manipulation

Sexual abuse is usually not the only way abusers mistreat their victims. Unfortunately, abusers are creative in the way they try to manipulate and control others. Most abuse survivors say things like this about the person who abused them:

"I was afraid of what he might do if I said 'no.'"

"He threatened to hurt someone else if I told what was going on."

"Sometimes he was really nice to me, like he really cared."

"He never talked to me when he was 'doing it,' as if it wasn't happening."

"He treated me like crap around my friends."

"When he drank, he became mean."

Sexual abusers almost always try to exercise emotional control over their victims. They may be intimidating or kind, frightening or unusually loving, emotionally distant or seductive, playful or demanding. There are all kinds of ways the abuser might manipulate a victim. Bouncing between normal, even loving behaviors and abnormal, even evil behaviors is a recipe for manipulation. The ultimate goal of the abuser is to create confusion in the victim. After all, a confused person can be taken advantage of more easily.

When trauma survivors look back on abusive experiences, they often express guilt, wondering how they could have allowed the abuser to take advantage of them. Yet, one thing that makes it so easy for abusers to mistreat their victims is that children are dependent on adults for so many things—they know that adults have a built-in advantage over them.

Emotional abuse takes on many shapes. Here are some of the more common forms:

- Neglecting to give you what you want or need

- Placing unreasonable demands on you

- Intentionally saying or doing things that upset and confuse you

- Preventing you from seeing your friends; isolating you

- Telling you what to say if people ask questions

- Buying you gifts to keep you quiet

- Putting you down in front of others

Recovery from abusive mistreatment involves freeing yourself from the emotional chokehold someone else may have on you. Abuse causes young people to feel that something is wrong with them. The truth of the matter is that it was the abusive treatment that was wrong, not you!

What Do You Think?

Read each of the following true-to-life cases. Describe how the adult might have emotionally manipulated the child and how the child might have felt.

Jennifer's Story

Jennifer's mother had a new boyfriend. When he first moved into the house, Jennifer liked him. He seemed cool. But soon he began to boss Jennifer around and before long he took charge of disciplining her. Jennifer complained to her mother, but she wouldn't listen. Within a few months, the boyfriend began to touch Jennifer where he shouldn't. When she protested, he punished her even more. Jennifer was trapped. He sexually abused her for more than a year.

How did the mother's boyfriend emotionally manipulate Jennifer?

_____

_____

_____

_____

How did Jennifer feel? In what way was she trapped by the abuser's manipulation?

_____

_____

_____

Tamara's Story

Tamara and her best friend, Deidra, hung out together every weekend. Whenever Tamara spent time at Deidra's house, Deidra's uncle came over and did favors for them. He took them to the mall and bought things for them. Tamara liked him. Once when she spent the night at Deidra's house, the uncle took her into a bedroom and molested her. At first she was scared, but when it was over, he treated her like a princess, just as he always had. The same thing happened two more times. Tamara wanted to tell someone, but didn't know what to do.

Was Deidra's uncle sincere in treating Tamara so well? How did he emotionally manipulate her?

_____

_____

_____

_____

How did Tamara feel? Why do you think she was so hesitant to tell someone that this man was abusing her?

_____

_____

_____

_____

What are some ways girls can keep people from manipulating them?

_____

_____

_____

_____

Think About It! All young people hope that their life is successful. They want to be successful in relationships, successful in school, successful in a job, successful in raising their own family. To wish for success is natural and good. Success comes when a young person recognizes who she is, aims at reasonable goals, and sets out to be her own person. Past manipulation does not close the door on future success.

Behavior Watch: Confused About Sexual Things

Sexual abuse is hard enough to overcome without being confused over sex. You may wonder, "What's right for me? What's wrong? Am I going too far?" Consider these guidelines:

- If you feel uncomfortable with a potential partner, don't get involved.

- If you think most people will frown on your decision, take time to think about what you are doing. The other people may be right.

- Healthy sexuality has little to do with short-term pleasure. It has everything to do with long-term commitment. Is your sexual behavior aimed solely at immediate pleasure? If so, tread carefully.

- Most teenagers think they are more prepared for sexual activity than they really are. If you're "raring to go," you're probably not ready.

- Teenagers who move slowly in becoming emotionally involved with others tend to find more pleasure than those who go too far too fast.

Useful Tip

Don't use sex as a way of meeting your emotional needs. Some abuse survivors become sexually active to show how angry they are at what happened to them. Others use sex as a way to prove to themselves and others that they have power over people. Learn to view sex as it is meant to be: a loving response between two people who have a lasting commitment to one another.

The Good Life

How do you define "the good life"? Many young people say that life is good when they have lots of trendy clothes and money, or more friends than they can count, or plenty of influence over others, or power and fame. Maybe these things are fine, but those who live the *real* good life are the ones who face life's struggles and emerge on the other side as a better person.

Let's be honest. Life is difficult. Perhaps one of the greatest lies we repeatedly hear is that life should be easy. Just watch a few TV shows. Read a magazine. Go to popular hangouts. The message is all around: *For life to be good, it should be easy.* That is simply not true.

Take note of what happens to those teenagers who constantly chase "the good life":

★ They value things over people.

★ They act the way they think others want them to act.

★ They throw tantrums when things don't go their way.

★ They try to ignore the unavoidable traumas that enter their world.

★ Relationships tend to be superficial and self-centered.

★ By ignoring life's stressors, they allow depression and emptiness to creep in.

While no one hopes for hard times, an unavoidable truth is that we all experience them. Some relationships fail. People mistreat, even abuse, other people. Children are taken advantage of. Divorce shakes a family's foundation. Not everyone can afford fine material things.

Those who experience "the good life" are the ones who refuse to give in to trauma and hardship. True happiness comes when . . .

◇ You give of yourself to another person

◇ You properly stand up for your own rights and needs

◇ You make peace with your past, no matter how troublesome

◇ You build lasting relationships

◇ You make the world a safer place for those who will follow you.

Sound Off

What are some ways movies, TV, magazines, and advertisements promote a distorted idea of "the good life"?

_____

_____

_____

_____

_____

_____

Finish this sentence:

My life would be better if . . .

_____

_____

Tonya's Story

A family member sexually abused Tonya for three years before she revealed her secret and the abuse stopped. By the time she was older, she was hurt and angry that life had treated her unfairly. She tried everything she could to force happiness into her life—she partied hard, took chances, indulged in sex, did whatever she could to make a fast dollar. And still she was unhappy.

Based on her behavior, how do you think Tonya defined "the good life"?

_____

_____

_____

What was missing in Tonya's search for happiness?

_____

_____

_____

What do people need to experience "the good life"?

_____

_____

_____

_____

Think About It! The good life does not mean partying "24/7" or sitting on top of an emotional high. Time is short. Chasing the good life in hopes of finding the ultimate thrill is like being a dog chasing its tail in vain. The good life comes when you find peace with yourself, when you love yourself. When life is good, you want to share it with others. To be fully you—*that's* the good life.

Behavior Watch: Grief

Most teenagers don't think of the word "grief" when they consider the aftereffects of sexual abuse. But abuse survivors should grieve. If a survivor does not grieve, depression, anger, anxiety, or fear may become intolerable. The good life will seem to be galaxies away. Hurtful grief can be overcome when you . . .

- Tell the story of your ordeal. You may not want to tell your story all at once, but do be open about talking to trusting and caring people.

- Keep a daily journal of your feelings. Write down what "triggers" you to have negative emotional reactions.

- Say goodbye to the person who abused you. Say goodbye to the lifestyle that shattered you. As if the past has died, allow yourself a fresh start at life.

- As much as you can, try not to blame yourself for what happened. Heaping blame on yourself for what someone else did gets you nowhere.

- Look into the future instead of the past. Write down realistic goals that you can accomplish in the next few days, weeks, months, and years.

Keeping Secrets

Most abuse survivors don't especially enjoy talking about their experiences, which is certainly understandable. But teen survivors who grow emotionally can eventually discuss their trauma. Telling the personal story of abuse is usually healing. In fact, many teenagers swear that each time they tell their story, they feel stronger. As healing as personal disclosure is, such conversations are not pleasant. For that reason, many victims keep their story secret.

One of the most destructive stumbling blocks to emotional healing is the refusal to talk about the pain of abuse. A surprisingly high percentage of teenage sexual abuse victims reveal their trauma to no one. Secrets can gnaw at a survivor's heart and soul, simmering like steaming water inside a boiling pot. The reasons for keeping secrets are many and include . . .

- Embarrassment over being involved in something "dirty"

- Not wishing to relive past tragedy

- Trying to avoid making waves with family members or friends

- A desire to "look good" in the eyes of others

- Fear of being misunderstood or—worse—talked about

- Not knowing how to bring up the topic

Other adolescents disclose that they have been abused, but when offered opportunities to heal by participating in therapy, support groups, or healthy family discussions, they skirt real issues. Though the *big* secret is out, plenty of small secrets remain hidden. While many of the above reasons also apply to this form of camouflage, additional explanations include . . .

- ★ Playing the role of "nice guy" by helping others instead of focusing on self

- ★ Rationalizing that "that was then, this is now"

- ★ Kidding self into believing that talking about abuse only makes matters worse

- ★ Feeling guilt over taking advantage of others' kindness

- ★ The helpless feeling that change will never happen no matter how hard the effort

The effect of past trauma lingers in all survivors. Those who can be open about their life experiences eventually learn to be completely themselves and allow love its proper space in their lives.

Your Thoughts

If you had to guess, how common is it for abuse survivors to keep secrets? What do *you* think is the main reason abuse victims keep their experiences to themselves?

_____

_____

_____

_____

What are the benefits of talking about your traumatic experiences with someone who can be fully trusted to help?

_____

_____

_____

_____

It is neither safe nor wise to talk to just anybody about your past. What qualities do you look for in a person before you talk openly?

_____

_____

_____

_____

Have you ever suspected that someone somehow knew your secret? How did you feel? What made you feel that way?

_____

_____

_____

What advice would you give a trauma survivor who is just now entering the healing process?

_____

_____

_____

_____

Think About It! There are times when troublesome thoughts should be removed from your mind. A teenager can stew over worrisome matters for too long. But the best way to deal with most emotional problems is to think about them, make sense of them, and work to become a better person. Tackling tough personal problems "one day at a time" helps you gain control over events you did not want to happen.

Useful Tip

Ask these questions when deciding who to talk to about your trauma:

- *How well does the person seem to understand my situation?*
- *Does she really listen to what I have to say?*
- *Can I say what I need to say without feeling looked down on?*
- *Does she let me express myself completely before offering advice?*
- *Can she be trusted?*

If you can answer "Yes" to all of the above questions, it's probably safe to proceed and talk to the person you have in mind. If you answered "No" to any one of the above questions, tread lightly.

Voices of Victory

After he did it he used to tell me that if I told, I'd be in big trouble. He said he'd kill me, or tell my mother it was my idea. He threatened to do it to my sister if I told. So I kept my mouth shut until one day a friend told me her secret. It was almost exactly the same as mine. That gave me the courage to tell her. Then I told an adult. If I had known how much better I would feel after telling, I would have told my secret much earlier. And when everyone found out who did it to me, he didn't dare come around me again.

—Rachel, age 15

Denying Damage

Closely related to keeping the abuse experience secret is the denial that the trauma did lasting damage. Not only do those who deny keep their experiences hidden from others, they keep their experiences from themselves! When you think about it, this practice is the ultimate put-down because it cheats the survivor out of the chance to bring a tragedy into the open so that healing can happen. And if the survivor denies herself the opportunity to heal, she cheats herself out of the chance for action. Teenagers who deny inner damage suffer as badly as those who admit their abuse but fight the healing process. Unconvincingly they may say to themselves and others . . .

"I don't know why, but I just don't get angry about those things."

"Yeah, I was abused, but it's nothing to get upset over—it happened!"

"He (abuser) was a jerk, but he's not worth fretting over."

"It won't happen again."

"I've handled my problems privately. I know what I'm doing."

"I'm not the type to give in to my feelings."

Just like cancer eats away at the body from the inside, denial of emotional pain eats away at a survivor's body. Some physical reactions include . . .

Difficulty relaxing	*Sleep problems*	*Startle responses*
Body tension	*Stomachaches*	*Restlessness*
Stress headaches	*Loss of appetite*	*Loss of energy*

Other reactions are emotional . . .

Chronic depression	*Worry and anxiety*	*Attachment difficulty*
Bitterness	*Mistrust*	*Low self-esteem*
Suicidal thoughts	*Quick temper*	*Loneliness*

Like cancer cells, secrets will not be denied the chance to do their damage. If not brought into the open, they seep out in hidden ways. One way or another, the secret will prevail.

What's Your Perspective?

Many trauma survivors have a "sixth sense" when it comes to spotting other survivors who are keeping secrets from themselves and others. Can you tell when a friend might be hiding a secret? What do you look for?

_____

_____

_____

_____

Respond to the following True/False statements:

T   F   Most survivors who keep secrets "pay" for their denial one way or another.

T   F   Practically every abuse survivor keeps *some* things from herself and others.

T   F   When a survivor denies her pain, she is allowing the abuser to have power over her.

T   F   As time passes, the damage of denying past abuse fades away.

T   F   Denial is a way to keep emotional pain from taking over the survivor.

Examine your responses to the above statements. What is your opinion about a survivor's need to talk about her experience?

_____

_____

_____

It is normal to deny an abusive experience for a while. Most survivors are stunned for a time after the abuse has happened. Eventually they let themselves think about what happened and then talk about it.

What are some feelings a teenager will probably have the first time she openly talks about her experience?

_____

_____

_____

It is normal for victims to "clam up" and quit thinking about their abuse from time to time. This can also be a form of denial. What are some reasons many victims weave in and out of denial?

_____

_____

_____

Think About It! Hard as it sounds, the healthiest teenagers are open with themselves about everything life has thrown their way—the good and the bad. Trusting yourself includes believing that you can grow through all of your experiences. It may take the help and support of others, but in the long run you are a better person for listening to yourself and becoming the person you want to be.

Behavior Watch: Taking Control of the Past

It's not enough to survive the trauma of sexual abuse. You want control over it. To feel that you are in control of your little corner of the world gives you a sense of security, a feeling of safety. You are in control of your place in the world when you:

1. Name the event that causes you trouble.
   I was sexually abused by _____ (fill in the blank).

2. Identify the feelings connected to the event.
   I feel _____ (fill in the blank) because of the events that shaped my past.

3. Decide how you will act from this day forward.
   I plan to _____ (fill in the blank) to show that I can grow in spite of what happened.

Survival is not enough. You want to know why you feel the way you feel, think the way you think, and act the way you act. Self-control belongs to you, not someone else.

Voices of Victory

I'm a control freak. My friends make fun of me because I'm a perfectionist. Only one of my friends knows my secret. The rest of them—well, it's none of their business. They wouldn't understand. I'm trying hard to quit being a freak about controlling things, if you know what I mean. I can be in control without going nuts about it. At least that's what I'm trying to do. I'm getting there.

—Tonya, age 17

Being Completely Young

Have you ever thought about what it really means to be young? Adults tend to look at teenagers as if you are strange aliens from another planet. What do they know! Most teens enjoy being young. In fact, the chances are good that one day you'll look back on these years and wish to be swept back to the days of your youth. (It's a middle-age thing. You'll understand one day.)

Depending on which expert you talk with, adolescence generally runs from eleven years old to twenty-one. At its best, adolescence can be . . .

★ The time of your life

★ A chance to try to discover the *real* you

★ The first time you are independent

★ An opportunity to make your own money

★ A chance to make new friends

As fun as the years of your youth can be, going through the trauma of sexual abuse can make a mess of "the best years of your life." Abuse survivors feel robbed of the fun their friends seem to have. The burden of abuse can result in . . .

◇ Broken relationships at home

◇ Feeling "different" and left out of the peer group

◇ Having to move around to get away from the abuser

◇ Going to see counselors and doctors

◇ Worrying about what your friends will think if they learn about your past

The years of your youth do not have to be spoiled because of your bad experiences. Believe it or not, plenty of your friends are in the same position you are. Sexual abuse affects as many as 25 or 30 percent (maybe more) of all girls by the time they reach age eighteen. When adults look back on their youth, they often remember that the best times of those years happened because they learned to give and receive support from friends who were going through experiences similar to their own.

Having Your Say

When you were a kid, what did you think being a teenager would be like?

_____

_____

_____

Now that you are a teenager, how have you been surprised by what you've experienced so far?

_____

_____

_____

What do you consider to be the best and worst things about being a teenager?

Best   **Worst**

1._____   1._____

2._____   2._____

3._____   3._____

4._____   4._____

5._____   5._____

Finish the following sentences:

Some things I have missed out on because of my trauma are:

_____

_____

_____

Some ways I am a stronger teenager because of my trauma are:

_____

_____

_____

Think About It! Too often we assume that the teenage years are nothing but one storm after another. It doesn't have to be that way. Adolescence is the last stage of childhood. But unlike young children, teens have the tools to decide for themselves who they will be, regardless of the past. Being "the best" does not mean winning every race, knowing everyone in your peer group, or making the highest grade. Being the best means that you choose to be truly yourself.

Useful Tip

Too many teenagers think that for the teenage years to be considered to be "good," smooth sailing is a must. The smart teenager is the one who considers life to be good when she figures out who she is and where she plans to go, no matter how many curve balls she's been thrown.

Voices of Victory

When I started treatment, they told me it would help if I told my story. I tried, but all that made me do was cry—cry and get angry all over again. So they suggested that I also write down my feelings and I did that, too. That helped. For one thing, it made it easy to tell people because I had already thought through everything. For another, I could write in privacy and didn't feel like people were looking straight through me as I unloaded all the things I've been through.

—Ashley, age 14

Anger Gone Mad

It is certain that you will feel anger toward the person who abused you. Anger is a good emotion when used the right way. It protects you from further harm and helps you correct all those horrible things that are wrong. It pushes you to stand up for what is right and good. Contrary to popular belief, anger is your friend. You need to be angry.

As healthy as anger can be, it is probably one of the most misunderstood of all emotions. People are afraid of the effects of anger, and rightly so. When anger is misused, it has tremendous destructive power. It affects a teenager's emotional and even physical health.

Anger is a tricky emotion. Used properly, it is a great tool for recovery. However, anger that goes too far becomes madness. You've heard of the "mad scientist" and "mad cow disease." Madness is usually associated with something other than constructive anger. Madness is associated with destruction . . . rage . . . fear . . . hatred. Madness suggests . . .

- ◇ Craziness
- ◇ Excessive fearfulness
- ◇ Loss of control
- ◇ Worry about little details
- ◇ Irrational thinking
- ◇ Panicked reactions
- ◇ Racing thoughts
- ◇ Loss of control
- ◇ Terror
- ◇ Revenge

Of course, no one is suggesting that you should not get mad about what happened. But there's a difference between "getting" angry and "going" mad. One is an act of courage and the other is an act of fearfulness. We like to make jokes about mad scientists and mad cows. Such talk is fine when it's confined to cartoons or wisecracks or funny stories. When madness is used to describe the reaction of an abuse survivor, it's not nearly as humorous.

What's Your Perspective?

Stan's Story

Stan was angry about just about everything. He didn't like girls because it seemed that too many of them tried to take advantage of him. He was angry at his mother for being such a weakling. He didn't like the kids at school because they seemed fake. One night Stan had taken just about all he could stand. He trashed his bedroom and fought his brother when he tried to stop him. He demanded that everyone in the house leave him alone. After the explosion was over, he found a piece of glass and carved the word "hate" on his arm.

Was Stan right or wrong to feel angry about his life situation? Explain.

_____

_____

_____

_____

In what way did Stan's "madness" make things worse rather than better?

1.

2.

3.

4.

5.

If you could give Stan some advice on how to better use his anger, what would you tell him?

_____

_____

_____

_____

_____

Assignment

The next time you witness a person (or yourself) going "mad," ask yourself what happened, why the person felt so angry, how his anger was destructive, and how anger might have been used more effectively. You can learn a lot when you think about what you see.

Think About It! Anger is not all bad—really! It does have a positive use. When teenagers get angry, it's because they are standing up for what they believe is right. A lot of good things happen when people stick up for themselves. But the truth about anger is that the way a person handles this emotion says a lot about what she thinks of herself. Anger and self-esteem are closely connected. Show that you like yourself by learning effective ways to stand up for yourself without being destructive.

Voices of Victory

If I had to say what being abused did to me, it would be that it ripped apart my self-esteem. I remember that before it happened I felt pretty good about myself, but after it happened and then it happened again, I felt dirty and basically worthless. My counselor told me that I had exactly the same amount of worth in me after I was abused as before. I thought about that for a long time and finally realized that he was right. And then I found the courage to love myself for the first time in six years. Let me tell you, it felt great!

—Elle, age 17

Useful Tip

After your next anger outburst, ask yourself some tough questions: *Are you just doing what you've seen other people do when they get mad? Did your outburst keep you from getting your message across? What's hiding behind those angry feelings? How can you say what you want without going overboard?*

What did you learn from your answers?

Overdoing It

Once sexual abuse is over (and even while it is ongoing), it can cause the survivor to experience imbalanced sexual feelings. Some sexually abused teenagers report that they are completely disinterested in sexual contact with the opposite sex. Others say that no amount of sexual contact will satisfy them. One girl will hardly talk with boys. Another won't go a day without a boyfriend in her life.

In trying to get rid of the hurt caused by one form of abuse, victims may find themselves trapped in unwanted cycles of sexual excess, which is an odd form of self-abuse when you think about it. Sure, the abuse victim may say she's not overdoing it and may claim she can stop these excessive behaviors whenever she wants, but too often she is only kidding herself. Any time teenagers become caught up in an imbalanced lifestyle, they are making a statement about what's missing in their lives. Consider the following behaviors of excess and possible statements the victim might be making through those behaviors:

Behavior	Statement
Behaving seductively	*I want to be in control of males.*
Many sex partners in a short time	*I won't let myself fall in love—ever!*
Wearing overly sexy clothing	*Someone please tell me I'm attractive.*
Deliberately covering the body with oversized clothes	*You'd better not look at my body like "that."*
Ignoring same-age males	*I'd rather be dead than trust a male again.*
Seducing, then "dumping" boys	*You hurt me, I'll hurt you.*

When abuse victims relate to males with excessive behaviors, they are not really stating their opinions on sexual matters. They are making a statement about how they think and feel about themselves and others. Here's a general rule of thumb that almost always holds true: *The way a person relates sexually to others provides a true picture of her overall emotional health.* That's a very personal statement (to say the least), but when you think about it, it makes sense.

Your sexuality is at the root of interpersonal relationships. If you have been hurt in this most personal way, it's hard to expect you to walk away from your experience without it affecting how you think, feel, and act toward others. Becoming aware of who you are as a sexual being can keep you from overdoing the way you relate to the opposite sex.

What Are Your Thoughts?

When you think back on your experience of abuse, how did it change the way you think of your-self sexually?

_____

_____

_____

How did your experience change the way you think about the opposite sex?

_____

_____

_____

_____

Reality check. Do you overdo your sexuality in any way? If so, what? If not, what are you doing to stay "sexually healthy"?

_____

_____

_____

_____

What comes to your mind when you meet someone of the opposite sex for the first time?

_____

_____

_____

I show my anger about sexual abuse by . . .

_____

_____

One way I can bring my sexual feelings under more balanced control is . . .

_____

_____

Think About It!

To feel close to people—not just members of the opposite sex but *all* people—you must trust them before you can feel close to them. People prove themselves to be trustworthy (or not) over time. Being open to another person does not require you to immediately become sexual. At the same time, for closeness to ever happen, you must eventually expose your true feelings—to yourself and to the other person. As you feel comfortable with yourself as a survivor, you will find that relationships take on new meaning and bring greater happiness. Let time be your friend.

Voices of Victory

You don't even want to know how many boys I've been with. It's embarrassing. I was first abused when I was six years old. It happened on and off until I was eleven. Since then I haven't been abused, but I became sexually promiscuous. I'm not sure which is worse: someone abusing me, or me abusing myself by acting like a slut or something. It makes me angry that someone showed me what sex is when I was so young. I probably wouldn't have been the way I am if I hadn't been abused. Sex is a good thing, but only if you use it the right way. Believe me, I know.

—Amberlee, age 17

Mad? Don't Kick the Cat

If you have been through any kind of abusive experience, there is no question that you will experience an emotional reaction—probably a strong one. People close to you may try to understand why you are upset, but then tell you to try not to be angry "all the time." You respond to them by saying that you simply can't help it. You're mad and can't get over it. Maybe you don't even want to get over it. But perhaps you feel that something's wrong because you are constantly agitated about something. For no real reason, you blow up over seemingly little things. For example, maybe you . . .

◇ Snap at a friend when she makes the slightest mistake

◇ Yell at your parents when they tell you "no" (and then you yell at them some more)

◇ Quickly fall into a bad mood when things aren't going your way

◇ Throw things or kick things or slam doors—and then wish you hadn't

◇ Make sarcastic remarks to friends or family even though you know they don't deserve it

◇ Refuse to do your schoolwork even though you could fail the class

When you have been sexually traumatized, you are going to experience anger. It is not wrong to feel this emotion. In fact, it is right to be upset about what happened to you. Something terribly wrong happened, and you want to make things right. The anger that results from an abusive event does peculiar things to a survivor. Not only is she angry at whomever mistreated her, she seems to be angry at everyone else, too.

Grabbing Hold of "Mad" Anger

Not all people are bad. Truth is, most people want to help others. Their motives are usually positive. They may not know what happened to you and thus cannot understand why you are grouchy and suspicious and moody and explosive. Even if they do know what you've been through, chances are that they don't quite know what to say or how to help you. When an abuse victim strikes out at a person who had nothing to do with her trauma, it is equivalent to kicking a cat as a way of taking out your frustrations. Cats don't deserve a fast kick in the side—and neither do people who want to help.

As you move beyond your abusive experience, it is important to ask yourself questions about how you are responding to your past experiences, questions like . . .

Who is my anger really aimed at?

When is the best time to tell others exactly what's happening inside me?

Am I being honest with myself and others in the way I communicate?

Am I taking out the feelings I have for my abuser on other people?

How are my emotions keeping me from receiving the help and support I want and need?

Your Turn

Think back on a time when you became overly upset at a person or group of people. What was the situation?

_____

_____

How did you overreact? What did you do and say?

I did these things . . .   **I said these things . . .**

_____   _____

_____   _____

_____   _____

_____   _____

_____   _____

When I overreact to others, they probably think these things about me . . .

_____

_____

_____

_____

What I really want people to understand about me is . . .

_____

_____

_____

_____

Others are more likely to help me through my ordeal if I choose to . . .

_____

_____

_____

_____

Think About It! It is not inappropriate for you to be upset about being mistreated. In fact, it is right for you to feel angry or hurt or any other protective emotion. When you become angry for seemingly no reason, or if you blast others when a milder reaction would have been more effective, examine yourself. Ask those tough questions that help you become more aware of the effect your experiences are having on you. Your emotions are intended to help you, not make matters worse. Use them wisely.

Behavior Watch: Anger Management

Anger is not such a bad emotion. (Heard that before?) Used correctly, anger can cause good things to happen. "Good" anger results in healthy changes. Take an inventory of your anger. It is good if you . . .

- Express your thoughts and feelings *without* the intensity of a raging bull

- Refuse to let your feelings build up until they come out in one big explosion

- Speak honestly, but respect the other person's feelings and opinions

- Give up your effort to win *every single* argument (It can't be done.)

- Pick your battles wisely

- Work hard at listening to what others say; if their words don't make sense, ask for clarification

- Remember that it's okay to walk away from a potential fight

- Don't worry about controlling others; just control yourself and your *influence* over others will rise dramatically

Soaked-up Memories

The very thought of your abusive experience is no doubt unpleasant at best, and it may even be downright nauseating. Abuse survivors develop various methods of coping with unpleasant memories. Some survivors take part in "behaviors of excess." A behavior of excess is exactly what the term suggests. It is a pattern of conduct that goes beyond normal limits. A general rule of thumb states that any imbalanced action results in a stronger than normal reaction, one that does more harm than good.

One of the most common behaviors of excess in abuse survivors is the overuse of illicit substances, especially drugs and alcohol. Even if you are not involved in either of these behavior patterns, you are at a higher risk than other teenagers for substance abuse at some time in your life. The stress of past abuse can drag a victim down to levels she might have thought she could never reach.

Drug and alcohol abusers who also have a history of sexual abuse reveal many of the following thoughts . . .

"Somehow when I'm drunk (or high) I feel more comfortable with myself."

"I know it's not good for me, but it helps me to get away from my stress, even if only for a few hours."

"I don't want to feel the things I feel. To be honest, I like being drunk."

"I don't know why I drink (or do drugs). I just do."

"The memories are so bad I can't sleep. Drugs (alcohol) help me out."

"When I'm drunk I can let go of my anger more easily than when I'm straight."

It's natural and even desirable that you are angry about what happened to you. You should be. Regardless of how right you are to be angry, though, drugs and alcohol do not help you cope with your trauma. They only make things worse. Consider these statements:

★ Alcohol/drugs do nothing to help you love yourself or others, and love is one of your greatest needs.

★ Alcohol/drugs cause people to have a distorted view of themselves and others at a time when "clear vision" is badly needed.

★ Alcohol/drugs prevent you from experiencing your real feelings, which keeps you from growing and getting better.

★ Being drunk/high only prolongs your agony. The escape you might feel while high is only temporary. The problem of dealing with past abuse will still be there when you wake up.

It's not fun to think about past abuse. And while it's not especially fun to work at getting better, the reward of defeating your abuser is worth the effort you make.

What Are Your Thoughts?

What percentage of abuse survivors do you think abuse drugs or alcohol? Is that percentage higher, lower, or about the same as for all other teenagers?

What is the most common reason you think abuse survivors might turn to drugs or alcohol to relieve their pain?

_____

_____

_____

_____

_____

What emotional or behavioral characteristics do you notice in young people who regularly abuse drugs or alcohol?

_____

_____

_____

_____

_____

In what ways does the use of drugs or alcohol actually make things worse for the survivor?

_____

_____

_____

_____

Instead of abusing drugs or alcohol, an abuse survivor can do the following things to relieve stress:

_____

_____

_____

_____

Think About It!

Sometimes it's hard to understand every emotion that surges through your body. Some feelings are harder to explain than others. But every emotion you experience is intended to help you, even the ones that seem to be negative. Rather than "soak" your feelings with an illicit substance, do all you can to be yourself—to feel your feelings. Being you is what recovery is all about.

Useful Tip

Learn all you can about drugs and alcohol. Learn about the effect they have on your body. Learn how drugs and alcohol affect family relationships. Learn what teenagers think when their friends develop substance abuse problems. Don't walk blindly into drug or alcohol abuse. Know what you're getting into. Learn that it's a game you can't win.

Voices of Victory

When you're sexually abused, you think that no one else has ever been through anything as bad as what you've been through. I was stunned when I learned that six other girls in one of my classes had also been molested or abused. I think it's terrible that so many kids are mistreated, but I've learned that when we stick together, we have power. Teenagers need to talk to each other about their feelings.

—Michelle, age 15

Who Are You?

—Just How Good Are You?—

One of the most important tasks in all of life is to discover "the real you." This task is not easy for anyone, and is especially hard for those who have been through trauma or hard times. Some trauma survivors say that life is one stormy time after another, and for some it is. But the smart young person is the one who tackles the job of defining who she is and where she wants to go in life.

Some people define themselves by their achievements. Their identity is based on what they have done. If these young people accomplish positive things, they see themselves as capable and good. For example, a person might define herself by saying:

"I made good grades in school."

"I'm good at dancing—nobody's better than me!"

"I'm the one who gets things done in my peer group. My friends come to me when they need a leader."

"I'm the one who keeps my family going when times get rough."

Others define themselves by their relationships. If they feel good about their family relations and friendships, then they feel significant. They might think:

"People seem to be attracted to me. I must be a likable person."

"I feel good about myself when I help a friend get through a rough time."

"I know I can count on my friends to pick me up when I'm down."

"My brother/sister knows what I'm going through and is always there with a helping hand."

There's another group of young people who feel confused. Rather than define themselves by what they have achieved or the relationships they have developed, they feel that they are not good at anything nor well liked by anyone. The experience of abuse pushes a young person to feel baffled about themselves. Confused teens may protect themselves by . . .

★ Isolating from others

★ Acting aggressively to vent personal frustrations

★ Allowing themselves to be controlled or dominated

★ Trying out exaggerated lifestyles

All teenagers feel confusion about some things. It is uncommon to meet a person who feels completely secure in her achievements or relationships. Identity development includes continually discovering and rediscovering your talents, forming relationships, and building confidence in yourself.

Your Reflections

Respond to the following True/False statements:

T   F   Children who are frequently praised for good behavior or positive achievement are more likely to feel good about themselves.

T   F   It is impossible for a young person to feel good about herself if her childhood relationships were stormy.

T   F   Negative behavior is always a sign of a person who feels badly about herself.

T   F   It is more important that a young person be liked by other people her own age than by older adults.

What do your responses to these items suggest about how you feel about yourself?

_____

_____

_____

_____

Write down several things you have done that you are proud of:

1.

2.

3.

What are some of your relationship skills?

1.

2.

3.

Assignment

In your quiet time, take a sheet of paper and make a list of at least twenty-five things you like about yourself. Your list may include things you have accomplished, ways you relate well to people, or personal characteristics you like. Share your list with a friend and ask for feedback.

Think About It!
The belief that you are valuable no matter what your behaviors and no matter the state of your current relationships is at the root of personal growth. Young people who are convinced that they have little or no worth are not surprised when bad things keep coming their way. Compare that to the young person who has learned to like herself, warts and all. When good things come to her, she is not surprised. She quietly says to herself, "Thanks, I deserved that."

Voices of Victory

I feel pretty sure that my mother knew that something was going on between me and her husband. I tried to drop hints but she would ignore them. I think that too many parents are afraid to admit that their kids might be being abused. I think abused teenagers should do what I did. I decided I wasn't going to take it anymore and I told somebody what was going on. Then I told my mother that I needed her to help me. When she saw that I could be strong, she became strong, too.

— Vicki, age 16

Your Body

It's almost scary how much emphasis society places on how a person's body looks—especially a female's body. Thumb through any magazine or view a movie and it seems that young, beautiful, skinny girls (and guys) are everywhere. Is that the way all of us are supposed to look? Of course not, but if you happen to be something besides beautiful and skinny, chances are you feel lacking in something.

If you were sexually abused, you are probably more aware of your body than those who were not abused. Why? When you were younger, one of the ways you learned about your body was through your interactions with other people. If people liked you despite your physical flaws and respected your right to control you own body, you were sent the message that you are "okay" as a person. If people took advantage of your body, you were sent the message that you are not okay as a person.

You may have felt a whole host of thoughts and feelings. Here are some of the experiences many abuse victims report:

◇ Feeling ugly or dirty because of what happened

◇ Feeling that every male (or even female) who looks at you is examining your body

◇ Wishing you could make yourself ugly so people wouldn't touch your body

◇ Punishing yourself through cutting or bruising or vomiting

◇ Wearing baggy clothes to disguise your physical features

◇ Flaunting your body since everyone seems to want a good look at it

◇ Making males pay (one way or another) to touch your body

As hard as it is, it is healing to become aware of how you view your body and how you present yourself to other people. After you have examined your own thoughts and feelings, it is useful to ask other people questions to see if they see you the same way you see yourself. You're almost certain to learn something valuable.

Do a quick check of yourself to see how you view your body. Ask yourself these important questions:

☐ Do you use your body to take advantage of people or get back at them?

☐ Have you deliberately tried to hurt your body because it felt like the right thing to do?

☐ When you are with others, do you wonder what they think about your body?

☐ Are you ashamed of the way you look?

☐ Are you too proud of the way you look?

☐ Do you dress so that people will ignore your body?

☐ Do you dress so that people will notice your body?

Becoming more aware of your body image can help you learn what it means to be you.

Look Inside Yourself

What parts of your body do you like? Why?

_____

_____

_____

What parts of your body do you dislike? Why?

_____

_____

_____

Get some feedback from a friend about your bodily likes and dislikes. Ask her opinion about your body, and tell her to be honest with you.

You may have heard the saying, "Clothes make a person." Do you agree or disagree? Explain.

_____

_____

_____

If your body could talk, what would it say to you?

_____

_____

_____

What are some ways you can be nice to your body over the next few days?

1.

2.

3.

4.

Think About It! Doctors say it all the time: "Listen to your body." Behind that statement is the message that a broken body cannot heal unless you pay attention to its needs. In the same way, a young person can observe (listen to) her body to "hear" what it is saying about her emotional health. Quite often, the clothes you wear, your outward presentation, even the food you put in your stomach are statements about your needs. What is your body saying to you? Are you listening?

Behavior Watch: Sexual Promiscuity

Sexual promiscuity is common in abuse victims. Many abused teens want affection and take sexual risks in order to find it. Promiscuous sex may bring momentary thrills, but virtually always it ends in disappointment, emptiness, and even shame. There are many ways to help yourself get over sexual promiscuity.

- Make a pledge to yourself to get out of and/or stay away from relationships where true love is not involved.

- Work to form friendships that do not require sex.

- Spend more social time in groups rather than one-on-one with a potential sexual partner.

- Do what you can to heal broken relationships with family and friends.

- Get involved in activities where you are required to help others. "Giving" to others does not have to involve sexual favors.

- Learn to identify early warning signs that someone wants to "use you." When you see those signs developing, turn and head in the other direction.

- Check the way you present yourself to others. If your dress, language, behavior, or attitude invites sexual advances from others, think about making changes.

Remember that sexual behavior does not always involve sex. Also keep in mind that another word for "promiscuity" is "carelessness." Be careful (not careless) in selecting your friends.

Voices of Victory

What do I think about the way teenagers dress today? It's like this: Boys try to look cool so girls will notice them. Girls try to look sexy so boys will drool over them. I ought to know—that used to be me. Then I stopped and thought, "Why do I want to look sexy for boys? I want a boy to like me for what's inside, not what's outside." So, I've quit trying to look like a beauty queen. I want to look nice, but I want to look respectable, too. Does that make sense?

—April, age 15

The Courage to Question

None of us knows what the future holds. It can be a frightening experience to look ahead one month, one year, or five years and think about what might be. Young people who grow emotionally don't dwell on the past. They look beyond the past and prepare themselves for the future. Sure, they run into doubts. They wonder if they're doing the right thing. They make mistakes.

As foreign as it may sound, asking questions is a sign of courage. It is only human to have doubts. People who "know all the answers" never grow. They are stuck with what they've always had. They are dishonest with themselves. They have trouble relating to others.

It is a mistake to "simply believe" that your world will get better. Trauma survivors who do not ask questions may . . .

Remain unsure of themselves

Never face their fears

Make the same mistakes over and over

Feel emotionally numb

Allow others to think for them

Feel stress building up inside

Experience physical and emotional pain

Every life is filled with uncertainty. A life that has been marked by abuse contains more uncertainty than normal. You might feel . . .

Guilty	*Frightened*
Alone	*Dirty*
Confused	*Insecure*
Ashamed	*Incapable*
Weak	*Disbelieving*

Asking questions requires hard work. But with hard work comes emotional maturity. That work can be done alone or it can be done with the help of others. No, it's not enough to "simply believe." You *learn* when you ask why. You become confident when you step outside your uncertainties. And most of all, each time you dare to ask tough questions, you discover that your doubts give birth to courage.

Sound Off

Think about the last time you were alone. No one was around. No one was watching you. No one could hear you. What do you think about when you are alone with your thoughts and questions?

_____

_____

_____

_____

_____

_____

Finish this sentence:

If I could, I would . . .

_____

_____

Take a True/False Test:

T   F   I feel funny when I find myself asking too many questions.

T   F   People tell me I'm an opinionated person.

T   F   It's easier to just wait and see what the future holds.

T   F   I like listening to people who tell me what to think.

T   F   It's best to just accept things the way they are.

T   F   I feel guilty when I doubt people that I want to be close to.

T   F   I run into the same problems over and over.

Examine your answers to the above statements. What can you learn about yourself based on your responses?

_____

_____

_____

_____

_____

Think About It! Most people ask questions in hope of finding answers. The curious thing about being sure enough of yourself to doubt is that the more "answers" you receive, the more questions pop into your mind. Doubting and questioning are necessary for growth. When you tell yourself, "I've found the answers," you immediately quit growing. Odd as it seems, for you to ever believe in yourself, you must constantly ask questions. Make a pledge to yourself that no matter if you are fifteen years old, or twenty-five, or fifty, or eighty, you will never quit having doubts and asking questions.

Voices of Victory

Oh, I've got lots of questions about my past. Most of them are about why this happened or why that person was such a jerk to me. There's no easy answer to those questions. If you get stuck trying to answer those questions, that's where you'll stay—stuck! If you ask other questions, like "Where do I go from here?" there's no end to what you'll discover.

—Julie, age 18

Learn How to Learn

Think about the person you are right now. You didn't become you all by yourself. Sure, you were born with a special and unique personality and part of who you are is based on those qualities. But much of who you are today is a result of what you learned from others about yourself. No one sat you down and gave you lessons about what it means to be you, but from the day you were born, you picked up cues from your world about yourself. You learned about yourself from:

⬦ The way people talked to you and the things they said

⬦ The moods people displayed around you

⬦ The way people touched you

⬦ The way people communicated with each other when you were around

⬦ The changes that happened during your childhood and adolescence

What you think about yourself is commonly called your self-concept. Your concept of yourself may or may not be accurate. If the words, moods, touches, communications, or events in your childhood came from people who deliberately or mistakenly sent negative messages, you likely came away thinking that you are not an especially good person. On the other hand, if your experiences were largely positive, the chances are much better that you learned the truth—that you *are* a good person.

One of the duties you take over as you grow older is to examine what you have learned about yourself and decide which lessons you learned are worth keeping and which need to be tossed aside. Simply because a parent or other adults or family members or peers say so doesn't make a lesson true.

- If you were abused by someone older and physically stronger than you, they were wrong.

- If peers or family told you that you are not as good as others, they were wrong.

- If you were made to believe that you can never amount to anything good, that is wrong.

- If people disapproved of you because you were not like them, they were wrong.

Learning about yourself is a lifelong exercise. You are not obligated to hold on to faulty lessons you learned as a child or teenager. Your self-concept is capable of constant change. It's something you can take charge of beginning right now.

It's Your Turn

Think back on your childhood and teenage experiences. What are some of the lessons you learned about yourself?

1.

2.

3.

4.

5.

Why do you think some people hold on to faulty beliefs about themselves, even though they know those lessons were wrong?

_____

_____

_____

Is it easy or hard to "relearn" lessons about yourself? Explain.

_____

_____

_____

What would you like to change about the way you think about yourself?

1.

2.

3.

4.

5.

Think About It! By the time you reach your teenage years, you know yourself better than anyone else. We sometimes mistakenly assume that our parents, friends, or other people can read us like a book. They can't. We sometimes mistakenly think that because someone says something bad about us, it must be true. Maybe it's not. If someone criticizes you, ask yourself, "Is he correct in what he thinks about me?" If so, accept his comment and use it to become a better person. If not, then do what you can to prove him wrong. Healthy people do that. A mistake that too often leads to self-esteem problems is to assume that others know you better than you know yourself. They don't.

Useful Tip

Only you know the real reasons you act and think the way you do. Be honest with yourself and others. You'll be saving yourself plenty of heartaches. Playing games with people only prolongs your pain.

Voices of Victory

I was so angry that no one could stand to live with me. I told everyone who tried to get close to me that I hated them. One way or another, that's the message I gave everybody. When a girl has been sexually abused she probably hates herself more than she hates other people. She doesn't know what to do or where to go. Anger is not so bad. It made me finally take a stand. I know I overdid it, but there's no way I would apologize for being angry at what happened.

—Tory, age 16

——What Other People Say——

You don't have to live long with sexual abuse to realize that most people who have not experienced what you have simply do not know what it is like to be in your shoes. Some people really do seem to understand you and genuinely want to help. Those are the friends and adults you should turn to for help. But many teenagers and adults have no clue what it must be like to endure sexual abuse. Whether they intend to or not, their words or actions can hurt. Some of the things misunderstanding people might think about you are . . .

"If you hadn't acted the way you did, the abuse never would have happened."

"Surely you could have kept the abuser from going as far as he did."

"Only 'bad' kids are abused. (Therefore you must be bad.)"

"There's a good chance you are exaggerating how bad your experience really was."

"You will probably end up doing the same thing to other people."

Maybe the easiest thing to do to people who completely misunderstand is to give them a piece of your mind or say something to hurt them just so they can catch a glimpse of how it feels to be inside your body. That kind of revenge might feel good for a moment, but it probably won't make things better in the long run—and it may even make things worse.

It is natural to want others to think highly of you. It is normal to want to correct people who have misconceptions about you. At times you will succeed in changing others' thoughts about you, but you can bet that you will be unable to get through to some people. You can talk until your face turns purple and they will still cling to faulty beliefs.

One of the greatest guidelines any trauma survivor can live by is simple but surprisingly hard to follow: *The highest form of evaluation is self-evaluation.* That plain statement contains mountains of truth . . .

★ Personal peace comes to you when you are honest with yourself and others.

★ You are capable of trusting your own experiences.

★ You know yourself better than anyone else.

★ The truth generally comes out in the long run.

★ It is always best to simply be yourself rather than what others want you to be.

★ When you are not threatened by what others think, you are showing your strength.

★ When you honestly evaluate yourself, you will find yourself more accepting of others.

★ Inner honesty is the surest way to personal growth.

We all want other people to have the right idea about us, but when you go through the unavoidable experience of being misunderstood, remain honest with yourself. You can be your own best friend.

Your Reflections

What are some opinions people have about you that are untrue?

_____

_____

_____

_____

When you know that a person misunderstands you, how do you usually react? Is your reaction helpful or hurtful?

_____

_____

_____

_____

What are some things about sexual abuse that only a survivor can understand?

1.

2.

3.

4.

We've all heard that child's rhyme, "Sticks and stones may break my bones, but words will never hurt me." Unfortunately, words _can_ hurt. In what ways have you been hurt by unkind words about your abusive experience?

_____

_____

_____

_____

Plan ahead by completing this sentence: The next time someone proves through their words or behavior that they misunderstand me, I will . . .

_____

_____

_____

_____

Think About It! It bears repeating that one of the greatest truths in all of life is that self-evaluation is the highest form of evaluation. Most teenagers are taught from an early age to pay too much attention to what others think. By becoming acquainted with yourself—perhaps for the first time—you may very well discover that what you think is better than what others say. Assuming that you are being completely honest with yourself, listen to your voice first.

Behavior Watch: Self-Esteem Problems

There's nothing that can tear down a teenager's self-esteem more than sexual trauma. Being violated in a sexual way can cause any girl to question her value. She might feel unattractive, unimportant, stupid, or worthless. Damaged self-esteem can be rebuilt.

- Be aware of the things you do that might cause people to look down on you.

- Take note of your positive traits. If you can't (or won't) identify any, ask others to help you make a list. You *do* have positive qualities. Everyone does.

- Learn to look people in the eye when you talk to them. "Smile" at others with your eyes. You'll be surprised at the pleasant reaction you receive.

- Volunteer to do something productive. Help your teacher. Tutor a friend. Send a "thinking of you" card to someone.

- Accept praise from people.

- Quit comparing yourself to the high school princess. She may not have higher self-esteem than you do.

When abuse and all the bad things that come with that experience have defeated a teenager, self-esteem problems can set in. Work hard to change what you think of yourself. You can turn negative self-thoughts into positive ones.

Useful Tip

At least twice a day, take the time to look in a mirror and give yourself a compliment. In fact, give yourself two compliments. Tell yourself how smart you are, how well you can sing, how you're proud of something you've done. It may feel funny the first time or two, but within a few short days, you'll look forward to seeing yourself again in the mirror.

Knowing You

One of the toughest jobs of being a teenager is discovering who you are. When you were a child, you probably didn't think much about why you did what you did or believed what you believed. (Life was simpler back then, wasn't it?) When you crossed over into that magical world of adolescence, you not only began to look like an adult, but you could think like an adult. Teenagers like to ask questions that begin with words like "what," "how," and "why."

"Why do I feel the things I feel?"

"What do I believe about drugs or alcohol or sex?"

"What will happen to me as an adult?"

"Why was I abused instead of someone else?"

"How can I become a better person?"

"What do I think about things like God and evil?"

"Why do adults make kids do what we do?"

The way you react to everyday events says a lot about who you are and what is important to you. When you think about it, it makes sense. You save your boldest reactions for the things you believe are important. By being aware of why you do what you do, you will be able to answer many questions about who you are as a person. Consider the following situations:

Situation:

Richard is with a group of teenagers and one particular guy is picked on unmercifully by the others. At first Richard joins in, but then he feels sorry for the boy. Richard takes up for him and tells the group to "back off." Richard's awareness of the other boy's feelings not only helped him be a better person, it made Richard think about the importance of befriending people even if they are different from everyone else. In the long run, Richard will not be as likely to treat others harshly because he is aware of his beliefs.

Situation:

Jennifer grew up around people who drank alcohol—lots of alcohol. In fact, when her mother's boyfriend got drunk, he often "messed with" her. As a child, she said she hated beer because it made people do bad things. One night when she has nothing better to do, Jennifer joins a few friends as they get "soaked." Afterward she feels kind of guilty, but rather than think about it, she gets drunk again the next night. The chances are strong that Jennifer will drift from one meaningless day to the next.

A first step in understanding who you are is to be fully aware of yourself. Too many teenagers are so busy paying attention to life's distractions that they miss great chances to learn about themselves. Teens who take the time to notice their reactions to everyday events become more completely aware of themselves. And self-awareness marks a big step toward answering all those questions that help you discover who you are. Teenagers who know themselves are far more likely to become satisfied adults than those who do not.

Think Hard

Think of a time when you acted in a way you wish you had not. You may have lost your temper, said something unkind, or deliberately hurt yourself or someone else. Whatever the situation, pretend you are in the middle of it right now. Answer the following questions:

Feel the *emotions* inside you. What are you *feeling* as you recall that situation? Are you feeling angry? Sad? Hurt? Confused? What are you *feeling*?

_____

_____

What *thoughts* are you *thinking* as you recall that situation? Do you think there's no way out? No one understands you? Life is unfair? Others need to feel as bad as you do? What are you *thinking*?

_____

_____

_____

_____

Can you think of other times when you feel and think similar things? Fill in the blanks:

Whenever I feel _____ or think _____ I am likely to _____

What have you learned about yourself? I am a person who . . .

_____

_____

_____

_____

Assignment

The next time you find yourself being something other than what you want to be, take yourself through an awareness check. What are you discovering about who you are?

Think About It!

A teenager is at her worst when she is acting—pretending to be someone other than herself. When teens pretend, they feel uncomfortable. Discomfort shows in the form of wild mood swings, irritability, depression, risk-taking, and many other imbalanced behaviors. A teenager is at her best when she is herself and no one else. She may feel confused at times. Her emotions may sometimes fail her. She will make mistakes. But above all else, she is true to herself. She never stops trying to become a better person.

Useful Tip

Now that you are capable of thinking like an adult, start thinking for yourself. Listen to what other teens have to say, but be smart enough to ask questions. Ask things like: *Who has to live with this decision—me or someone else? How is this going to help me in the long run?* You are your own person. Learn to think for yourself.

Voices of Victory

I like to think about everything. Thinking makes you wise. When you think about things, you see things that other people don't even know are there.

—Ashley, age 14

Going Underground

When life has done a number on a teenager, it is natural for that teen to somehow, some way try to get back at whoever hurt her. Retaliation can take many forms and it can be oh so sweet. Some abuse victims become very sly and subtle in the way they hurt others, to show just how strongly they feel about being hurt.

Any time a teenager shows her anger and hurt to others, relationships will be changed. If the teen goes underground with her emotions, others may have difficulty knowing exactly what she thinks and feels (which is the reason she went underground in the first place). Often, a teenager may become so skilled at hiding her true self from others that she ends up deceiving herself as well.

A teenager who is angry about her abusive past may show hurt feelings in these subtle ways:

⋄ "Accidentally" forgetting to do something helpful

⋄ Sexually teasing boys and then letting them go

⋄ Procrastinating just long enough to ruin someone's plans

⋄ Borrowing things and returning them in bad shape (or not at all)

⋄ Spreading gossip that you know will hurt

⋄ Omitting important details when passing along information

As you define who you are, honesty is necessary. As important as it is to be honest with others, it is even more important to be honest with yourself. Teenagers who are honest with themselves have learned that . . .

In the long run it is more satisfying to be completely "real"

Truth wins out over deception over the course of time

Others can sniff out deceit, and almost all avoid it

Forcing silent power over others is a sign of weakness more than strength

Personal honesty is a key ingredient to growth

Dig Deep

Think of a person with whom you are often dishonest. What are the reasons you hide your real self from that person?

_____

_____

_____

What do you *like* about deceiving that person?

_____

_____

_____

_____

How does it hurt you to be dishonest with yourself and others?

_____

_____

_____

_____

Name some ways you can be honest with yourself while at the same time protecting yourself from being taken advantage of by others.

1.

2.

3.

4.

Think About It! When you've been hurt, it's tempting to become something or someone you are not. After all, your experience has taught you that other people may take advantage of you unless you protect yourself. A basic task in growing stronger is to show your true feelings without causing constant conflict. To do that, it is necessary to be open and honest with yourself. Make a point to know who you are, know why you feel the way you feel, and accept yourself as a valuable person. Self-acceptance is the ultimate way to bring out the best of your personality.

Voices of Victory

I used to hurt myself. You name it, I did it. I cut myself with whatever I could find. I made myself get too fat. I made myself get too skinny. I got drunk. I got high. I let boys do things to me that the man who sexually abused me did. I finally got sick of it. I said to myself, "If you're doing all these things to relieve your pain, it's not working." Self-abuse is all about self-hate. I don't want anything more to do with that.

—Jodi, age 18

Let Them In or Keep Them Out?

If someone were asked to describe you, what would they say?

"She's quiet. It's hard to know what she thinks."

"She has a temper. It takes nothing for her to blow up."

"I can't say why, but she seems depressed."

"She acts like the whole world is resting on her shoulders."

"I don't know about her. She's a mystery to me."

"She's one person one minute and another person the next."

"You never know what kind of mood she's going to be in."

You are largely defined by the way you handle yourself. When others describe how you express your feelings, they are describing you. If your experience includes sexual abuse, how you express your feelings about being mistreated plays a role in how people see you. In other words, your abuse experience has become a part of who you are.

To say that your experiences define you can be a depressing thought. Being defined as "that abused kid" is not what you want people to think when your name is mentioned. It doesn't have to be. Instead, you can be defined by how you handle your emotions.

"She's quiet, but when she talks she seems confident."

"I've seen her get mad, but she handles things pretty well."

"She's been through hard times, but she's determined not to let it get the best of her."

"When she talks about the future she seems optimistic."

"She knows when to share her feelings with people."

"People know where they stand with her. She's dependable."

"You can depend on her to be the same person no matter what comes along."

When people are asked to describe you, they often describe what you do with your feelings. Of course, people will not know that you have been abused unless they are told. But your behavior will give others a hint about your life experiences. Your behavior also tells others whether you are taking charge of defining yourself or whether you are letting your experiences define you. Teenagers who have big blow-ups may be sending this message: *Life has treated me hard. I don't know who I am, how I feel, or where I'm going.* Teenagers who have learned to express their feelings appropriately rather than let them build may be sending a different message: *Life has treated me hard. I'm trying to figure out who I am, how I feel, and where I'm going.*

Take time every day to examine your emotions. Express them in a healthy way by talking to a trusted friend, writing in a journal, or creating an art project. It's up to you to decide who you are. Don't let your feelings dictate what kind of person you will be.

Having Your Say

What phrases do people use to describe you?

_____

_____

_____

_____

What phrases would you *like* people to use to describe you?

_____

_____

_____

_____

Kisha's Story

Kisha is friendly most of the time. She spends time with her friends, but claims that she's not really close to anyone. She was abused by her stepfather and is afraid that a few of her friends might know her secret. Just to play it safe, she never talks about her family and rarely lets her friends come over to her house. Many people would be surprised to know that Kisha is depressed and sleeps poorly because of bad dreams.

How would you describe the *real* Kisha?

_____

_____

_____

_____

How do her friends probably view her?

_____

_____

_____

_____

What advice would you give Kisha to help her be true to herself and others?

_____

_____

_____

_____

Think About It! Your friends want to know who you are. While everyone keeps certain parts of themselves private, it's okay to share your feelings with people. When a teenager bottles her feelings, she is not being to true to herself or others. By sharing yourself with friends you can trust, not only are you being open and honest, you are no longer sitting on a powder keg that's waiting to explode. By letting others into your world, you'll make your relationships fuller and more satisfying. What's more, you'll be content with who you are becoming.

Useful Tip

One of the best ways to show people that you are confident in yourself is to look them in the eye when you speak. Teenagers who look down or away when talking to friends and adults are telegraphing a lack of acceptance of themselves. Those who look others in the eye are making a positive statement: *I feel good about being me.*

Voices of Victory

I didn't want to look pretty. Pretty girls attract men and I'd had enough of that. But people kept saying to me, "You're pretty. You're pretty." Even when I tried not to be, they would tell me that. So I asked myself what does it mean to be pretty. It means that you love yourself and that your heart is clean. Now I know that I am pretty.

—April, age 15

It's Not Easy Being You

A temptation abuse survivors face is to ignore certain aspects of themselves. Of course, the part most abuse victims would like to ignore are the negative thoughts and feelings caused by their abusive treatment. To feel the anger and hurt and embarrassment and sadness of abuse is like being forced to swallow a bitter pill. It seems right to simply dismiss those feelings and to push positive emotions into their place. But it's not.

One odd truth about emotions is that people cannot select which feelings they will feel and which ones they will not feel. Put simply, if you feel angry, hurt, embarrassed, or sad, you cannot ignore it. One way or another, your emotions will find a way to be released. When survivors attempt to live out certain feelings and ignore others, they end up being someone other than who they really are. To be true to yourself, you must express *all* your feelings. Otherwise you are not being you.

When a survivor tries to hide certain parts of herself from others, several things may happen. If you ignore the troublesome side of your personality, negative emotions:

- Tend to grow stronger like an untreated cancer

- Build up and seep out in unexpected ways

- Cause you to deceive others into believing you are something you are not

- Require so much energy that positive feelings are ignored

- Keep your outward self and inward self from matching up, causing guilt or anxiety

- Create emotional numbness, potentially resulting in a stale feeling

When you think about who you are, you must consider all sides of your personality. All of your experiences and all of your emotions need to be dealt with in an open and honest manner. As unpleasant as it may be, being open to all of yourself helps you grow to be everything you are capable of being. When you are true to yourself, good things happen:

You feel "real."

Your positive emotions aren't overpowered by your negative side.

People are attracted to you because you are no longer putting on an act.

You feel like you have more energy—emotionally and physically.

The past no longer hangs over you like a dark cloud.

You find yourself capable of helping people who have been through experiences similar to yours.

Your Reflections

Name ten words other people probably use when they describe you:

1.   6.

2.   7.

3.   8.

4.   9.

5.   10.

Name ten words you *wish* other people would use to describe you:

1.   6.

2.   7.

3.   8.

4.   9.

5.   10.

Finish these sentences:
   A part of me I often ignore is . . .

_____

_____

_____

When I refuse to experience all of my emotions I hurt myself because . . .

_____

_____

_____

I intend to be true to myself by doing the following:

_____

_____

_____

Think About It!

Teenagers who try to be what they think others want them to be are not being themselves. They are only acting. When you do all you can to hide some of your feelings (especially the negative ones), you are keeping people from loving you. And the effort you give to hiding those negative feelings prevents you from loving others. In order to experience the emotion of love, you must let yourself feel afraid or angry or anything else that's in you. As soon as you let yourself feel all of your emotions, you become more aware of yourself. You are then free to grow.

Voices of Victory

Have you ever had to look in the mirror and you didn't like what you saw? I did. Every time I looked in the mirror, I would find something else wrong. I was never good enough. Eventually whenever I looked at myself in the mirror I tried to think of something nice, like "You've got a nice smile" or "That color looks good on you." I would actually talk to myself in the mirror. One day I even started to laugh at myself. I don't know why, but when I did I felt great. If you're ever going to get over your problems, you have to be able to look in the mirror and smile.

—Amberlee, age 17

The Wrong Rules

Everyone lives according to a set of rules. When you were very young, your parent or guardian probably made up rules for you, things like:

People are not for hitting.

Furniture is not for jumping.

Eat all the food on your plate.

Do what your teacher says.

And on and on. The rules a child must live by are many (probably too many when you think about it). When children reach adolescence, more rules are applied, "advanced" rules like . . .

No cheating on tests.

Obey all traffic guidelines.

Treat your elders with respect.

If you break something, expect to pay for it.

It may make you feel better to know that when you become an adult, rules will still wiggle their way into your life. You can't get away from them. But one of the nice things about growing older is that you get to make up rules that you believe to be important. Hopefully the rules you live by really will be advanced, such as . . .

Treat other people the way you like to be treated.

Give some of what you have to people who need it.

To make friends, be a friend first.

Gain influence over others by controlling yourself.

Teenagers often make rules according to their life experiences. If abuse has been a part of your past, you may find yourself living according to rules that may or may not be in your best interests, rules like . . .

Don't trust anyone of the opposite sex.

Don't make waves, just give in.

Life stinks anyway, so do what feels good.

Forget the other guy; watch out for your own back.

As you go through the challenging task of discovering who you are, take time to discover the rules by which you live. Keep an open mind in examining those guidelines. Remember that not all rules should be set in stone. As you change and learn more about yourself, the rules you live by should change with you.

What's Your Opinion?

What are some rules that teenagers in general are told to follow?

_____

_____

_____

What are some rules that the adults in your world tell you to follow?

_____

_____

_____

What rules do you choose to follow simply because of your past experiences?

_____

_____

_____

In your opinion, what rules would all people follow in a perfect world?

_____

_____

_____

Finish this sentence: I can use rules to help me become a better person by . . .

_____

_____

_____

_____

Think About It! If you are a teenager who believes that in a perfect world there would be no rules, you are not alone. Most people don't like to be told how to behave. But whether you act as you do because you are forced to do so or because you want to do so, you do follow a set of rules. To test a rule's value, ask if it helps you and/or others become a better person. If so, follow it. If not, do away with it.

Behavior Watch: Conduct Disorder

The word "disorder" sounds so bad! How can a person have a conduct disorder? Remember that a disorder is an extreme form of any emotion or behavior. In its simplest terms, a conduct disorder is a strong refusal to follow rules and reasonable expectations. You may have a conduct disorder if you:

- Fight or intimidate people
- Engage in illegal acts
- Don't care about the feelings of others
- Lie, cheat, steal, and swindle people for no real reason
- Refuse to see things through others' eyes

Most conduct-disordered teens are unhappy. They're hiding their feelings beneath a mask of toughness. Truly "tough" teenagers shed their masks and face up to life's problems.

Your Many Shades

It's natural for teenagers to experience mood changes from day to day. One day you're in a great mood and it seems that nothing can go wrong. On other days you don't feel so hot and it seems that more things go wrong than right. At the end of those days, you're happy to turn out the lights so you can wait for tomorrow. Everyone knows the feeling of good days and bad days.

Just like everyone else, survivors of sexual abuse report mood changes. However, rather than the normal ups and downs other teenagers feel, survivors often report that their emotions and behaviors seem to range far wider than what other kids experience. For example:

◇ *Not only do Hillary's friends wonder which personality she will show from day to day, she wonders, too. Her plunges into a foul mood are so unpredictable she sometimes wants to isolate herself from people altogether.*

◇ *There are days when Sharonda gets along just fine with her best friend. On other days, she yells and screams as if she's deliberately trying to start a fight.*

◇ *When Terry thinks about the past, he sometimes thinks he understands himself. At other times, the very thought of days gone by is enough to make him feel dizzy.*

◇ *Arnett promises herself one morning that she will make it through the day without worrying about little things. She does pretty well until about noon when something happens to trigger her anxiety. For the rest of the day she can't concentrate.*

Changes in your moods can cause you to wonder, *Who am I anyway?* The truth is, you are *all* those things you see in yourself. In the same way that you can be kind and understanding, you can also be rude and selfish. Just as you are confident in many ways, you doubt yourself in other ways. Sometimes you do a good job controlling your anger, sometimes you do a lousy job.

There are several reasons you may experience broad mood swings, including . . .

★ When survivors try too hard to stuff "negative" feelings, those same feelings may force themselves to the surface at unexpected times.

★ The belief that other people are in control of you keeps you from consistently expressing your true thoughts and emotions. At times, you simply can't resist the urge to cut loose and let others know where you stand.

★ In your desire to keep your friends from knowing all the embarrassing details of your life, you may try to be someone you are not. It's hard to keep up a front all the time.

★ Your angry and hurt feelings may make you feel defiant, so you show it. Afterward, guilt sets in and pulls you back to a more "civilized" way of behaving.

No one is black-and-white in their feelings and behavior. All people have good and not-so-good qualities. Knowing who you are and what makes you tick helps you become a balanced person.

It's Your Turn

On my worst days, I guess you might describe me as . . .

_____

_____

_____

_____

Not that I want to brag, but on my best days I am . . .

_____

_____

_____

_____

I can let my positive qualities shine more brightly by . . .

_____

_____

_____

_____

Ways I can better control the darker side of my personality include . . .

_____

_____

_____

_____

_____

What are some ways you can help a person who is struggling with mood swings? How could you help her be better balanced?

_____

_____

_____

_____

_____

Think About It!
Think of yourself as an artist's palette. You are a mixture of colors. You are not all black or white. Neither are you completely red or blue or green or any other color. You are a beautiful mixture of colors. Your dark moods need not overshadow your lighter feelings. When you do a good job of mixing the many shades that make you uniquely you, you will begin to take the form of a well-crafted work of art.

Useful Tip

Moodiness is a sure sign of hidden feelings. Trouble is, those moods are so potent that they refuse to stay down. They come out in the form of pouting or sarcasm or backstabbing. If people use the word *moody* to describe you, consider the possibility that you are hiding too many emotions—from yourself and others. Find the courage to open up to someone you can trust.

Voices of Victory

Maybe it's good when you feel numb after what happened. Don't get me wrong, you shouldn't deny being abused, but for a while I was so shocked that I kept telling myself that what happened wasn't real. For months I didn't know what was going on. When I was around my friends, the worst part of me came out because all this junk was inside me. I was losing friends right and left. But then I talked about it. I couldn't believe the words that were coming out of my own mouth. When I was asked, "Are you sure that's what happened to you?" I said, "Yes." At that moment I knew that it was real and I knew that I was going to win.

—Tonya, age 17

Managing Your Feelings

Is Life Worth Living?

Have you ever had that sinking feeling that life is not worth living? If so, take heart that you're not the only one. Many teenagers feel that way from time to time. Some even feel that way a lot of the time! However you answer the question "Is life worth living?," there is hope for you.

Let's look at some of the reasons trauma survivors might wish life would end.

⬦ Sometimes it seems that no one cares.

⬦ Life may be so stressful that you feel you can't take it.

⬦ You want to be with someone you love who has passed away.

⬦ You are convinced that the future will be as bad as the past.

⬦ You were abused and you're sick of it.

⬦ You feel that you deserve to be punished.

Young people who have overcome suicidal thoughts have several things in common. Listen to what some formerly suicidal people have said about how they defeated the urge to die:

"I quit blaming myself for everything that has gone wrong in my life."

"When I started helping others, I realized that people need me."

"I talked about my pain and someone listened. The pain didn't completely go away, but now I know that someone shares my burden with me."

"Instead of directing my anger at myself, I directed it at the person who hurt me."

"I learned that my future is more important than the past."

Q: Is life worth living?
A: You bet it is!

One important lesson about suicidal feelings is that it is okay to feel that way! But that doesn't mean you should act on suicidal thoughts. It simply means that there is probably a good reason that you feel devastated. Maybe you've been hurt by someone you loved. Maybe your life has taken a turn for the worse. Perhaps someone or something you loved very much is no longer there. Whatever the reason for your despair, it's valid.

When life hurts so badly that you don't want to go on living, consider these thoughts:

★ It may seem that these feelings will never go away, but with some effort they can and will.

★ Every time you resist the urge to hurt yourself, you have defeated whoever or whatever drove you to feel like you do.

★ The anger you feel means that something is wrong and you want to make it right.

★ Your life is valuable just because you are you!

Dig Deep

When you hear the word "suicide," what is the first thought that crosses your mind?

_____

_____

_____

If a friend says to you, "I feel like dying," what would you do and say?

_____

_____

_____

If you felt like dying, what would you want a friend to do and say to you?

_____

_____

_____

What are some reasons that so many trauma survivors feel that life is hardly worth living?

1.

2.

3.

4.

Finish the following sentences:

The next time I feel that life is hardly worth living, I plan to

_____

_____

One thing I can do today to make my life more meaningful is

_____

_____

Assignment

Can you think of someone who has been a help to you in the last few days? Come up with a thoughtful way to tell that person "thank you" (and then do it).

Think About It! It's too easy for a person to look at suicidal thinking as a "cop out" or a sign of weakness. It is not. Suicidal thinking is an expression of frustration, helplessness, anger, and sadness. Those who overcome suicidal thoughts have learned that no matter what their situation, how unfairly they have been treated, or how dreadful their experiences, they are in control of themselves. To love in spite of all else is the greatest gift a person can give herself. When a person loves herself, she discovers that life has meaning.

Behavior Watch: Suicidal Urges

Don't feel guilty if you experience suicidal thoughts because of your abuse. Sexual trauma can push you to the edge, making life seem as if it's not worth living. But don't give in to suicidal urges, either. Your life can always get better if you work at it. If you feel suicidal . . .

- Tell someone you trust how you feel. If you can't trust anyone, make an appointment right away with a school counselor, minister, or adult friend. Teens who tell others that they feel suicidal are strong, not weak.

- Enter into a contract with a helping person stating that you will not try to hurt yourself.

- If you need to be hospitalized, so be it.

- Work with a counselor and family members to develop a network of people you can rely on to encourage you. Meet with them regularly. You need support.

- Get involved with a group or organization that gives you a feeling of belonging. Teens who fit in with other teens are less prone to suicidal thoughts.

Useful Tip

Stand up for your rights. You don't have to be an ogre to be assertive. Any teenager can respectfully demand to be treated with dignity. Say what you mean. Mean what you say. Respect the rights and feelings of others. Doing these things helps to keep you from feeling used and abused.

—Unloading Personal Stress—

Stress is something that visits all teenagers. Words closely connected to "stress" include:

★ Depression   ★ Worry   ★ Bummed out

★ Pain   ★ Tension   ★ High-strung

Stressors can be small, but all those little irritating things can add up to make big headaches. Think of how often "little" stressors have affected you, things like . . .

◇ Realizing that you have no clean clothes to wear

◇ Losing your homework (The dog ate it!)

◇ Being late for an appointment

◇ Having to wait your turn to use the telephone

◇ Noticing one more pimple on your face

Stressors can be big, too:

• The separation or divorce of family members

• Suffering the trauma of abuse

• Moving away from close friends or family

• Witnessing domestic violence

• Finding out that you have a serious illness

Stress is a normal part of life. In fact, a certain amount of stress is healthy. Think about it—if you are happy-go-lucky and stress-free all the time, you have no reason to change and no motivation to learn new coping skills. For that reason, moderate stress is good. Of course, if stress becomes all too common in your life, it can be overwhelming. Stress is a peculiar thing. No stress makes life drab, while too much makes it unbearable.

When stress becomes difficult to manage, you might express it through exaggerated behavior. Highly stressed young people who act out may be sending messages like the following:

★ I'm not happy because I feel so misunderstood.

★ I want someone to step in and relieve the pressure I feel.

★ It's not fair that other kids have an easier life than I do.

★ I wish I could find a way to fit into a peer group.

★ I want some respect for the effort I've made.

Whatever your stress level and however you express it, you have the choice to better manage your emotions. Stress is a part of your life, but it does not have to defeat you—it can be managed.

Your Reflections

What are the greatest sources of stress in your life right now?

_____

_____

_____

_____

_____

What happens when teenagers try to ignore stress?

_____

_____

_____

_____

What are some of the negative ways you handle the stress in your life? (Be honest.)

_____

_____

_____

_____

What are some of the healthy ways you handle the stress in your life?

_____

_____

_____

_____

One recommended way to combat stress is to be good to yourself. How can you be good to yourself over the next few days?

1.

2.

3.

4.

5.

Think About It!

Stress can be another word for discomfort. We tend to shy away from whatever is uncomfortable. We even fear discomfort. Sometimes we call discomfort being "stressed out." We are upset because we are stressed out. We hurt people. We act ugly. We destroy things—all because we are stressed out. The truth is that people may act mean because they are afraid. Healing comes when we confront our fears rather than fighting them.

Voices of Victory

I know I used to think that no one can possibly know how I feel. I thought that I was the only one who went around stressed out all the time. That's not true. Some of the people who have helped me were abused, too. Some of them weren't. But all of them know what it's like to feel hurt or guilty. We're all the same when you think about it.

— Michelle, age 15

══Separation and Loneliness══

One of the most troublesome consequences of sexual trauma is the lonely feeling that lingers long after the abuse is over. Even years after the experience, many victims report that they still feel an emptiness inside their body. Sexual abuse is a highly personal event, so personal that it seems that no one else could possibly know how it feels afterward. It can cause you to feel separated from anyone whose experience is different from yours.

Young people who feel separated from others often report loneliness. Loneliness involves more than simply being isolated from others. People who are lonely may . . .

- ★ Talk to people without really saying anything

- ★ Try to deny the awful events of the past

- ★ Deceive others by acting as if they are something they are not

- ★ Force too much attention on themselves

- ★ Cut themselves off from people who care

- ★ Flit from one relationship to another without making a commitment

- ★ Act rude so that people will not like them

There are many reasons that trauma victims feel isolated. But to alleviate the pain of emotional loneliness, victimized young people need to allow themselves to be visited by others who truly want to help, people such as:

- • Those who have been through similar experiences

- • Understanding family members

- • Counselors and other helping professionals

- • Members of the clergy (ministers)

- • Close friends

Believe it or not, most caring people can tell if you are lonely. And if they truly do care, they wait until you are ready for their support rather than force you to accept it. Loving people do that. They wait, and they enter your world when you let them.

Many abuse survivors struggle with loneliness when they keep their feelings to themselves. They assume that sharing their emotions with others will not really solve things, so why bother? But those who find the courage to tell how they feel about things find themselves getting stronger. And as an added bonus, they report that people seem to warm up to them.

What's Your Perspective?

Love is one of those peculiar words that we all know how to describe, but ask ten people to define it and you may get ten different answers. How do *you* define love?

Some of the ways I keep others from giving me their care and concern are:

_____

_____

_____

_____

_____

What I really need from a friend or family member is:

_____

_____

_____

_____

_____

Plan Ahead

I'm going to be more open and honest with others by making three changes in the coming days:

1.

2.

3.

Think About It! What are your loneliest moments? If you are like many trauma survivors, you feel lonely when it seems that no one understands what you feel at that very moment. You are created for relationships. No person is meant to live an isolated life. The most rewarding times you will have are when you talk—really express yourself—to someone who listens. You may leave the conversation without coming to any conclusions, but the very fact that you have shared your inmost thoughts eases your burden.

Useful Tip

Initiate one meaningful contact every day. Make it a daily goal to approach a friend (or even someone you don't know all that well) and talk to them. Ask them about their interests. Get them to tell you about their activities. Try not to talk too much about yourself. Teenagers like other teenagers who are truly interested in them.

Who's in Control?

Control. We all want it, and sometimes we will do whatever it takes to get it. The word "control" takes on special importance if you have been through a sexually or physically abusive experience. Being abused causes you to feel that you have been robbed of control. It has been forcefully stolen from you.

When you are in control of your life, you feel comfortable, secure, important. The loss of control results in opposite feelings—discomfort, insecurity, insignificance.

Here's a curious truth about life: *The struggle to be in control of yourself can become so intense that you actually lose control.* Consider the following situations:

After being repeatedly told that she is fat and ugly, Yolanda stops eating so she can be thin and beautiful.

Anne wants to hurt the person who has mistreated her, but he is physically powerful. Instead, she cuts her body with sharp objects.

A normally compliant teenager shuts down when criticized for not working as hard as she is capable of working. Her shame leads to depression.

When people bear down on him with criticism, David "zones out" and daydreams about other things until the harassment is over.

Young people who cannot control the events of their lives often do whatever they can to stay in charge of their emotions. If they find themselves losing that battle, they may do what they can to bring others down to their level of frustration, anger, and disgust. While the feeling of revenge gives temporary satisfaction, the endless fight for control over others eventually takes its toll in the form of . . .

Failed relationships	*Constant fights*	*Frequent criticism*
Dishonest communication	*Lost friendships*	*Unending arguments*
Chronic stress	*A bad reputation*	*Bodily tension*

One of the simplest, yet greatest, truths of life is that the only person you can control in all the world is yourself. When you give others the right to make you depressed or angry or anxious, you are giving away personal control. Likewise, when you try to force control over others, you will lose your capacity to have a healthy influence on them.

Sound Off

Have you lost control? Take this simple test:

Yes	No	I have a hard time getting along with others.
Yes	No	People often say my behavior is too extreme.
Yes	No	I often wonder if people are working with me or against me.
Yes	No	Helpless feelings creep around inside me.
Yes	No	I blow my stack more often than I should.
Yes	No	I frequently second-guess the decisions I make.
Yes	No	I don't run my life—other people do.
Yes	No	Sometimes I do things for no other reason than to prove that I can.

How do control issues get in the way of your relationships?

1.

2.

3.

4.

5.

What do you think? Finish this sentence: Ways I can better control myself include:

_____

_____

_____

_____

_____

Assignment

Over the next few days, make a point to honestly observe the way you try to control yourself and others. Watch what happens when you make positive adjustments in exercising self-control (and learn from your observations).

Think About It! When you try to control another person, three things might happen. The other person might give in and allow you complete control. She might compromise and allow you partial control. Or, she might resist and give you no control at all over her. In any case, the relationship won't work. When someone tries to control you, you can give in, compromise, or be your own person. You manage your emotions best when you remain true to yourself. You don't try to control others. You don't let them control you.

Behavior Watch: Controlling People

Controlling people are really not much fun to be around. Sure, they may be in charge of what's happening, but control freaks are usually lonely people. You are a control monger if you:

- Argue just for the sake of arguing
- State your opinion when no one asks for it
- Blame others for whatever goes wrong
- Insist on having the last word

The only person in the whole world you can control is *you*. If you do a good job of that, you don't need to control other people—your influence will be strong enough.

Voices of Victory

I don't remember too much about my childhood. I'd rather forget as much of it as I can. I'm getting better now that I can face up to my problems. I don't shove aside what happened yesterday, mostly because I don't have to. What happened yesterday wasn't so bad because I made an effort to have a good day. No one is hurting me now because I'm out of a bad situation. I'm in charge. I'm in charge of what I do, what I think, how I act, and what I remember.

—Elle, age 17

Getting Angry (Is Okay!)

Here's a statement that we can all agree upon: All people get angry. Even the best people are angry from time to time. Anger is a natural occurrence. It happens to everyone.

If anger is so common, why does it have such a bad reputation? No doubt, the fact that so many people (especially young people) use anger in a destructive way causes it to be the "bad boy" of emotions. But used correctly, anger is healthy. Consider these observations about anger:

Anger is an emotion that every person in every corner of the world experiences.

Anger can be witnessed in the youngest infant and the oldest adult; it is lifelong.

Anger is a response to bodily tension, discomfort, or frustration. It is natural.

Anger's message is: Something is wrong and needs to be made right.

Anger is a necessary agent for change.

It is unfortunate that anger has gained such a negative reputation among emotions. Too often we are told, "Don't be angry." In truth, anger is an emotion that protects the human body and soul. Maybe people should be told, "Be angry, but be angry in the right way."

The experience of sexual abuse brings out a whole host of emotions, and anger is probably at the top of the list. Being traumatized in this way certainly causes a tense reaction in your body. It creates all kinds of discomfort—physical, emotional, and even spiritual. It leaves you feeling frustrated. Something is terribly wrong in the experience of sexual abuse and needs to be made right.

If anger is such a good thing, why does it seem to drag so many teenagers down? Consider these guidelines:

◇ Think about your anger rather than simply acting on it. Explosive anger is not nearly as effective as controlled anger.

◇ Learn to listen to your body. Too often abuse survivors try so hard to stuff their anger that their body rebels. If you have frequent headaches, stomachaches, insomnia, or other physical discomfort, ask yourself if anger is involved.

◇ Learn to state your feelings in a controlled manner. Anger's message tends to become lost when it is surrounded by noise.

◇ Refuse to feel guilty because you are angry about what happened to you. Look at your anger as a helpful tool rather than a destructive force.

Where Do You Stand?

Take a personal inventory of your anger . . .

I am angry about:

_____

_____

_____

_____

Things I would like to see changed are:

_____

_____

_____

_____

The person (or people) I am most angry with is (are):

_____

_____

I am angry at this person (these people) because:

_____

_____

_____

Name some of the ways you misuse your anger (and then try to correct them):

1.

2.

3.

4.

5.

Think About It! Anger is all about survival. Put simply, if you *never* feel angry, you will be figuratively "eaten up" by someone or something. Anger is normal. But the single most destructive thing that turns anger into a sour emotion is selfishness. Selfish anger seeks to slam other people, to put them in their place. Selfish anger looks for revenge. It tries to win at all costs. The trouble with selfish anger is that it breeds more selfish anger. For anger to be good, it must be used and then put away for another day and time.

Useful Tip

Most angry teenagers don't like being mad all the time. Anger is not an especially fun emotion. Be smart enough to recognize when you've crossed the line into damaging anger. Take a time-out to be alone. While alone, think about things. Think deeply. What were you trying to communicate? Where did you go wrong? Is it worth it to fight with the other person? Where is your anger taking you? What's a better way to get where you want to go?

Voices of Victory

A year ago, if you had told my friends that Tory was this laid-back girl, they would have said, "Yeah right. That girl's crazy." They were right. "Crazy" means that you have these feelings inside and don't know what in the heck to do with them. So you just blast everyone with everything you've got. People who aren't crazy know what it's all about. Yeah, they get mad the same as I used to. They just get mad the right way. People respect you when you get mad in the right way.

—Tory, age 16

──Someone's Mad (at You)!──

It seems that adults talk a lot to young people about how to control themselves when they are angry. Handling your anger is probably one of the best relationship skills you can develop. Everyone gets angry from time to time, so it's good to know what to do when that time occurs.

But what happens when you're doing a good job handling your anger while someone else is blowing up—and you're the target? Most young people defend themselves and may even retaliate with their own anger. Of course, that does little more than cause a bad situation to get worse—fast!

It takes some heads-up thinking when someone gets angry at you, but with some planning and practice, you can not only prevent a disaster, your influence over the other person can become surprisingly strong.

When you are the target of someone else's anger . . .

Do	**Don't**
Try to keep your cool	Immediately blow up
Recognize that the problem may not be yours	Assume that you are in the wrong
Try to size up whether the person is interested in your side	Spout off to a person who will not listen to you
Communicate in a friendly manner	Act just as angry as the other person
Choose the right time to give your feedback	Say what you think right then
Exercise your right to leave the conversation	Hang in there way too long
Think about what was said afterward	Think about how to get even
Make logical choices about your next step	Act impulsively without thinking

If you have endured traumatic relationships in the past, chances are good someone has inappropriately displayed anger toward you. Another person's anger can hurt you, intimidate you, pull you into unnecessary fights, or keep you feeling stressed. Your response to other people's anger, whether they are adults or teenagers, says volumes about your strength as a person. Of course, you're going to make mistakes and react more strongly than you should from time to time. But by becoming aware of how another person's anger affects you, you can keep it from controlling you. While it may not be apparent at the time, when you show strength and poise in response to anger, you are decreasing the chances that bad scenes will happen repeatedly.

Dig Deep

Be honest with yourself as you complete this sentence: When someone gets angry with me, I usually . . .

_____

_____

_____

_____

_____

Jan's Story

While at school Jan approached Joan and verbally lit into her, accusing her of "talking trash" about her earlier that day. Joan felt that Jan was blowing the entire matter out of proportion. She wanted to give Jan a dose of her own medicine by sarcastically reminding her that she had a reputation for being the worst gossip in the school. Instead, she waited until Jan was through ranting and said, "I don't agree with you, but I refuse to talk about this while you're so angry." Jan ranted some more and eventually walked off.

What do you think those who witnessed Jan's anger thought about her?

_____

_____

Who did they see as being more "in control" of herself—Jan or Joan? Explain.

_____

_____

Joan should be congratulated because . . .

_____

_____

What advice does Jan need to hear? Explain.

_____

_____

Think About It!

The word "control" is a key word in relationships. People who feel unsure of themselves need to control others. Likewise, people who allow themselves to be controlled by others are insecure. Teenagers who are truly "in control" do not attempt to dominate others and do not let others dominate them. They realize that by staying in control of themselves, they are showing strength. It is those teenagers who have a healthy influence on their peers.

Useful Tip

It's really hard to tell an abuse survivor that pain is good. It's not. Emotional pain causes discomfort that hurts every bit as much as the worst physical pain. Discomfort causes a person to want to be better. So, in an odd way, pain is a motivator. Use your pain as a reason to make a better way for yourself. Ease your discomfort by spoiling yourself today. Do something fun you wouldn't ordinarily do—and don't feel bad about it.

Voices of Victory

Don't tell me about pain. I know what pain is all about. It's about being mad and hurting so bad that you might explode. It's about wanting to curse God. It's about hating everyone. It's about deciding that you won't take it anymore. It's about making decisions. It's about moving ahead. Pain is about getting better.

—Vicki, age 16

Feeling Frozen

It's hard to know what to think about being abused. Something bad happened. It makes no sense at all that a perpetrator would take advantage of a child, but he did. In the same way that it's hard to know what to think about abuse, it's also hard to know how to feel. Many abused teenagers don't know if they feel mad or sad or hurt or dirty or afraid or all of the above. Some survivors report that they feel nothing at all. They feel emotionally limp. Abuse can bring about a numb feeling.

Like all emotional reactions, the numb feeling that follows trauma has a positive purpose. Frozen emotions help keep the victim from further harm. When a trauma survivor turns off her feelings, she is doing what she can to prevent further pain. It's like going to the dentist and taking a shot of anesthetic before the drilling begins.

While there may be temporary benefit from "freezing" your emotions after a terrible event has happened, at some point in time those emotions need to be thawed out. Otherwise, personal growth stops and relationships become empty. Those survivors whose emotions remain frozen might say the following . . .

"I may act like I care about people, but I really don't. I don't want to be close to anyone."

"I pretend to be happy, but on the inside I feel nothing."

"People tell me they love me. Yeah, right. They just want something from me."

"I learned a long time ago that feelings only make you hurt."

"I do things to get back at the people who hurt me—and I don't feel a thing."

Those teenagers who break out of the destructive cycle that started when they were abused say that they have to make themselves learn how to feel all over again. Like a little child who makes sense of words like "love" and "fear" and "happiness" and "anger" for the very first time, successful survivors must go through a process of learning the meaning and purpose of their emotions. Those who do say things like . . .

"I feel alive again for the first time in years."

"It's like I've learned to appreciate the little things in my life again."

"Now I want to help someone make it through their pain."

"I can't believe how creative I became once I let myself feel what's inside me."

Your Reflections

Try to think of a recent time when you felt emotionally numb. What was the situation?

_____

_____

What happened inside you?

_____

_____

How did your frozen emotions help you through an awful experience?

_____

_____

In what ways are you hurting yourself by not allowing yourself to be open to your emotions?

_____

_____

_____

_____

Finish the following sentences.

I'm going to be open and honest when I'm with _____

                                        (name a person you can trust)

Being open with this person will help me by _____

_____

The next time I find myself retreating to "the deep freeze," I will _____

_____

Think About It! There is no acceptable answer to the question "Why was I abused?" Try as we may to find a reason for such tragedies, we cannot. A survivor can only look for responses, not answers. You can respond to your trauma by loving yourself, by helping others, by forgiving the world for not being perfect. Trauma should not freeze your emotions. You are free to go about your life in spite of—and maybe even because of—your experiences.

Behavior Watch: Frigid Feelings

Ever been around someone and felt that she was "ice cold"? Ever been accused of being frigid? Frigid teenagers are hurting. They hide their feelings by:

- Refusing to talk about anything important

- Deliberately provoking people to keep them at a safe distance

- Clamming up when everyone else opens up

- Trying to convince themselves that they are strong when they aren't

- Putting emphasis on things rather than people

Emotionally frigid teenagers are usually without meaningful friendships. They are more likely to develop headaches, stomachaches, and other assorted aches. It takes courage and hard work to "thaw out," but in the end, the results are satisfying.

Voices of Victory

I really love my counselor. I never knew it could feel so good to just talk and know that the person sitting across from you understands everything you're saying. She can't solve my problems for me. I know that. She just helps me be me! It's the best feeling in the world because I'm not frozen anymore.

—Vicki, age 16

—What, Me Worry?—

Anxiety is a common response to sexual trauma. Anxiety is a complicated emotion. Tangled up in this single experience are worry, fear, depression, physical discomfort, tension, and more. Anxiety seldom happens without reason. In the case of sexual abuse, the victim was violated, so anxiety developed to cause her to be cautious and to help keep her from being hurt again. Like anger, anxiety is a protective emotion.

Anxiety can be experienced in a teenager's mind and body in many ways . . .

◇ Physical restlessness

◇ High heart rate or blood pressure

◇ Difficulty relaxing; bodily tension

◇ Stomachaches or nausea

◇ Nervous habits

◇ Inability concentrate

◇ An assumption that the worst will happen

Anxiety can affect a teenager's relationships. You may . . .

◇ Bicker with people over senseless matters

◇ Become overprotective

◇ Feel emotionally stiff

◇ Find your feelings are easily hurt

◇ Be overly critical of yourself and others

◇ Become unable to handle pressure from others

◇ Assume people do not like you

The trouble with anxiety is that it feeds on itself. When a teenager gets into a cycle of anxious thinking, one worried thought leads to another and then another. The emotion that started out as a protection from harm can destroy your self-confidence and prevent you from forming valuable friendships.

Used correctly, anxiety helps a teenager . . .

◇ Think before she acts

◇ Move slowly into new relationships

◇ Become properly aware of her own and others' motives

◇ Make informed choices

◇ Plan ahead for what might happen

◇ Keep from being taken advantage of

Having Your Say

All people experience anxiety. Some people have more anxiety than others. How does anxiety show up in you?

_____

_____

_____

_____

In what ways does anxiety get in the way of your relationships?

_____

_____

_____

_____

_____

Anxiety has protected me in the following ways:

1.

2.

3.

4.

Assignment

The opposite of excessive anxiety is relaxation. Think about it. You cannot be tense and relaxed at the same time. Name an activity you will do in the next day or two to help you relax.

_____

_____

Think About It! To hear someone say, "Don't worry, things will get better" may not be especially comforting. We all worry. Perhaps it is better to hear the words, "I understand your worries. What can you learn from your anxiety?" Anxiety's aim is to encourage caution. It is not meant to tie you up in knots and keep you from being content with yourself.

Useful Tip

You can't be tense and relaxed at the same time. To relax, take time every day to scan your body. If you feel tense, close your eyes. Pretend that your arms and legs are so heavy you cannot possibly lift them. Let the muscles in your face go limp. Imagine that your stomach is completely empty. Take several deep breaths. It feels great to be relaxed. It also helps you feel in control of your emotions.

Voices of Victory

I was scared. I mean I was really scared. I could hear him walking down the hall to my room and I knew what came next. I laid there stiff as a board and hoped that this time he would leave me alone. It never worked. But it's over now. I can breathe again. I still get these panic attacks, but I tell myself again and again, "It's over now. You can breathe."

—Annie, age 15

The Takedown

Emotional pain wears many different clothes. People normally assume that teenagers who are hurt and saddened because of hard times will cover themselves in depression and hide by emotionally withdrawing from others. Fact is, abuse survivors who feel emotional pain are just as likely to show their hurt in a loud, boisterous manner. As if they are in a wrestling match with all the world, they wish to take down as many people as they can so everyone will know exactly how enraged they feel.

The hurt caused by emotional trauma can put blinders around the victim's eyes. Unable to see anything but their internal misery, they fail to recognize that not everyone will hurt them. Even when friends or family members or professionals offer much needed aid, the blindly hurt teen may reject it. Worse, she may do all she can to pull others down to her level. It is as if someone must pay for what the abuser did. That old saying "Misery loves company" holds true.

Many traumatized young people receive an odd enjoyment at pulling others to their level of hurt. They may think or say . . .

"I've been insulted and I want people to know that I'm not going to take it anymore. If people think I won't fight back, they're wrong!"

"When he abused me, he obviously showed that he didn't respect me. So why should I respect anyone? Let them see how it feels!"

"I stay mad all the time, especially when I think about what happened. You may think I'm weird, but I feel really good about myself after a good fight, especially when I win!"

"I've tried being nice. I've even apologized for something I didn't do! That didn't work, so now I'm doing what I want to do until I get the apology I deserve!"

"You say you understand me. How can you understand if you haven't been through what I've been through? Why don't I show you exactly what it's like. Then maybe, just maybe you'll see what it's like to be me!"

"I see people who look happy and act like there's absolutely nothing wrong in their life. That makes me sick! How can they act like that when I'm going through so much hell?"

A hard lesson to learn in overcoming deep emotional wounds—especially wounds that were caused by someone else—is that emotional "takedowns" prevent young people from recovery. For each person taken down, the survivor prolongs her misery. To look at it another way, every person who is dragged down to your level of pain is unable to lend a hand to help you up.

It's Your Turn

Honesty time. Read the following statements and answer True or False as it applies to you.

T	F	It bothers me to see people act so happy when I feel so upset.
T	F	I get this strange feeling of satisfaction when I make another person feel like I do.
T	F	Sometimes I just don't care what happens to other people. I've got enough troubles of my own without worrying about them.
T	F	I don't want to talk about how I feel. I'd rather show it.
T	F	I agree with that phrase, "I don't get mad, I get even."
T	F	If I show other people how I feel and it offends them, that's their problem, not mine.
T	F	Most of my life I've felt weak because I was abused. For just a few minutes, I'd like to feel stronger than everybody else.

When I examined my answers to the statements above, I learned this about myself:

_____

_____

_____

Rather than take others down to her level of pain, a trauma survivor should . . .

_____

_____

_____

Ways I would like to change the way I express my hurt are:

1.

2.

3.

Think About It! There's an old saying that "Only the strong survive." A song has even been spun from those words. Strong people are not the ones who can overpower others. Strong survivors have an inner peace that no matter what pain they have been through, they know they're going to make it in life. Internal strength is more often seen in who you are rather than how loudly you speak.

Behavior Watch: Defiance

If anyone has a reason to fight the world, it is a traumatized teenager. The anger, hostility, and unfairness of abuse are enough to cause anyone to want to fight back. While it's good to stand up to those who hurt you, defiance can be so strong that it tears relationships apart and makes teen life even harder. To guard against damaging defiance, you can . . .

- Talk to trusted friends or adults about the hurt and anger that make you want to fight.

- Make a list of the things you can truly control, and then work to control those things.

- Give up trying to control what other people do. (You can't control anyone but you.)

- Make a decision to do at least one favor for someone every day. By giving to others, you are doing more to make your world right than you will ever do by fighting.

- Even if you think your parent's (or other adults') rules are senseless, follow them. You'll be given more freedom if you respect authority.

- Make a list with two columns—one that lists how you feel and one that lists how you behave when you feel that way. Make a connection between your feelings and your behavior.

- Think of several recent defiant episodes. Ask yourself what happened afterward. Determine a better way to communicate with the people with whom you are upset.

Voices of Victory

These are some of the things I know: I know that I'm a good person no matter what happens to me. I know that I'm going to make it. I know that I'll never abuse anyone the way I was abused. I know that I need help and I'm not afraid to ask for it. I know that I did the right thing by finally telling my story. I know the future will be as bright as I make it.

—Jodi, age 18

Dammed Up

It's amazing how differently abuse survivors handle their experience. Some are quite vocal in expressing their feelings. Others are not. Some actively think about what happened to them. Others do their best to forget the whole thing. Some write down what they think and feel. Others are numb to their thoughts and emotions.

Any extreme form of emotional expression is damaging and keeps a teenager from growing to be all she can be. Just as it's damaging to blast others with your anger, so too is it harmful to keep your experience completely to yourself. In the same way that building a dam along a river creates a backlog of water, containing your emotions at all costs results in a buildup of emotions. Somehow, some way, those emotions will be expressed. If you don't let them out in an open, honest fashion, they'll come out in a hurtful, disguised way.

Some abuse survivors can go weeks, months, or even years without talking about the feelings that are attached to their abusive treatment. They may succeed in fooling others into believing that everything is all right, when in fact everything is anything but all right. Survivors may even go so far as to make the following claims:

"Nothing's wrong. I just don't feel like talking."

"I got over the hurt a long time ago. There's no need to talk about it anymore."

"I handle my emotions best when I deal with things on my own terms."

"You may not believe it, but I've almost forgotten that it happened."

"I've seen other girls fall apart when they talk about their abuse, and I'm not interested in that happening to me."

In their refusal to talk about their emotional pain, these survivors may be doing the *opposite* of throwing a temper tantrum. In the same way that the loud, defiant survivor wants to force control onto her world, the stubbornly quiet teen may be stating . . .

"I don't want my abuser to know how badly he hurt me."

"I think I'm safer if keep my feelings to myself."

"I tried once before to tell people what's going on inside me, but it backfired."

"I can't punish the person who abused me, but I can punish everyone else by refusing to let them into my world."

A refusal to talk about an abusive experience can be as damaging as blasting the whole world with your emotions. Hurt and angry feelings that are turned inward cause depression. When you're not honest with others (and yourself), relationships suffer. Physical discomfort may even increase. Being open with the right people is like releasing a flood of emotions that have been held back by an unnecessary dam.

Being Honest

What percentage of your thoughts and feelings do you share with people who want to help you? Make a mark on the line below.

0% _____ 50% _____ 100%

What excuses have you heard teenagers use for refusing to tell others what they really think and feel?

_____

_____

_____

Maria's Story

Maria looks and acts pretty much like any other teenager. What people don't know is that an adult "friend" of the family sexually abused her. She doesn't want anyone to know about this for fear of what they might think or say. A couple of her friends are aware of her secret and want to help. Likewise a few adults know about Maria's situation and have told her she can talk with them any time she feels the need. But instead of appropriately using these people to help her through hard times, she chooses to clam up.

What might Maria say or do to convince her friends that she doesn't need their help?

Maria might say the following . . .

_____

_____

Maria might do the following . . .

_____

_____

How is Maria hurting herself by refusing the help of others?

_____

_____

What advice would you like to offer Maria?

_____

_____

Think About It! It's always a risk to tell someone what you think or feel. But teenagers who grow through emotional trauma are smart risk-takers. That is, they are wise in building a network of friends whom they can trust. Sometimes that network includes other teenagers. Sometimes it includes family members. Sometimes it includes a therapist or counselor. The feeling that comes to a survivor who shares her emotions with the right person is one of release. To allow a caring friend into your world means that you don't have to face the burden of pain alone.

Behavior Watch: Sexual Arousal

Sex is a good thing. (Say that out loud in a group of adults!) True as that is, sometimes adults send teens the opposite message: *Sex is a bad thing.* It's not. Of course, candy is good, but too much can rot your teeth. When does a teenager cross the line from normal (healthy) sexual arousal to abnormal (unhealthy) sexual arousal? Consider these guidelines:

- It is normal to have thoughts, dreams, or wishes about sexual things. By themselves, these things do not hurt people.

- To act on your thoughts, dreams, or wishes is another thing altogether. Before you act, be sure to consider the consequences of your behavior. If what you do in any way causes discomfort to you or someone else, stop.

- Normal people masturbate. If you do, don't feel guilty. If you do it a lot, consider the possibility that your emotional needs are not being met.

- Be careful about movie, music, or magazines loaded with sexual themes. You really can get too much of a good thing.

Voices of Victory

I've tried everything—drugs, sex, alcohol, partying. None of it made me happy. I quit talking to my mother because she blamed me for being abused—as if it was all my fault. I hated life. Then I started thinking, "I don't just hate life. I hate myself." That's not right. A girl shouldn't hate herself just because she was abused. No way! She should love herself. When you love yourself, you don't need all that other crap. Somehow, it doesn't mean anything to you.

—Rachel, age 15

———"Just Right" Feelings———

Remember the story of Goldilocks and the Three Bears? (Sure you do.) When Goldilocks raided their house and tasted the bears' porridge, one bowl was too hot, another was too cold, and the third was "just right." Which bowl did Goldilocks devour? She chose the "just right" bowl. She also chose the "just right" chair and the "just right" bed. Things were going well for her until she got caught. (Did you ever wonder if Goldilocks could be charged with unlawfully breaking and entering a house? Never mind.)

Like Goldilocks, people are attracted to things that are just right. If something is too hot or too cold or too hard or too soft or too anything, we tend to avoid it. Another lesson from this child's story is that balance is something to strive for. Not only should teenagers look for balance in "things" but in emotions, too. When your emotions are balanced, people are attracted to you. When your emotions are imbalanced, trouble lurks.

Your emotions may be "too hot" when you . . .

- Fly off the handle over the least little thing

- Rant and rave and use choice language to make a point

- Take every available opportunity to spread gossip about someone you dislike

- Sob and cry and moan and groan to manipulate others

- Insist on getting in the last word in an argument

Your emotions may be "too cold" when you . . .

- Hold a grudge against a friend or family member much longer than is necessary

- Give someone the silent treatment for days (or longer)

- Hold on to bitterness for so long that it's hard to love others

- Let mistrust build to the point that you feel paranoid

- Purposely turn off your feelings because you don't "need" them

Your emotions are probably "just right" when you . . .

- Use your emotions when the situation calls for it, but then let go

- Look back on troubling situations so that you can learn from them

- Stand up for yourself without destroying your reputation at the same time

- Speak the truth, but consider the other person's feelings, too

- Show a willingness to consider points of view different from your own

Maybe the story of Goldilocks and the Three Bears wasn't meant to be an illustration of how to go about properly managing your feelings, but the lessons fit. Use your emotions when the situation calls for it, but don't overuse them to the point that you are out of balance.

What Do You Think?

If the people who know you best (family and friends) rated your emotions, which ones would they say are "too hot"? Why?

These emotions are too hot . . .   **Because . . .**

_____   _____

_____   _____

_____   _____

_____   _____

In what ways would those same people say you are "too cold"? Why?

These emotions are too cold . . .   **Because . . .**

_____   _____

_____   _____

_____   _____

_____   _____

People whose emotions seem to be "just right" seem to have it all together in these ways:

_____

_____

_____

_____

Things I plan to do to express myself in a more understanding way are:

_____

_____

_____

Think About It! "Balance" is one of those words that most anyone can define, but it's so hard to reach. Balance means being honest with yourself and others. It requires that you look at all sides of an argument. It expects you to forgive yourself and others for things that have gone wrong. With balanced emotions, you are more likely to succeed in your teenage years—and beyond!

Behavior Watch: Fighting Your Impulses

Life has been hard. Maybe you wish to strike back. Striking back can mean taking risks—risks that could hurt you or others. Impulsive behavior can include anything from spontaneous "fun" to carelessness to self-abuse to thoughtless sex. You can fight your impulses by . . .

- Agreeing with parents, other adults, or even friends on reasonable rules that are intended to reduce risky behaviors

- Talking to others about the fear, anger, and even sadness that pushes you to be careless (Remember that "careless" can mean "I don't care about myself")

- Dressing and acting in ways that suggest that you are not seeking attention

- Avoiding saying and thinking negative things about yourself and others

- Thinking about the consequences of your behavior before you act, and assuming that the worst may very well happen

Most teenagers don't connect impulsive behavior and past sexual abuse, but the truth is that the two too often exist side by side. Controlling impulses involves more than following rules and accepting limits. It requires that you seek safer—and more healing—ways of expressing your thoughts and feelings.

Voices of Victory

I used to hate myself because I believed him when he told me it was supposed to feel good when he did sexual things to me. It did feel good, but I didn't want it to. But feeling good is more than just what your body feels. Feeling good means that you're being respected. Sexual abuse is not what it means to be respected. Your body is not lying to you when it does what it's supposed to do. It's the abuser who's the liar. He doesn't respect you.

—Amberlee, age 17

Relating to Others

Your Personal Independence Day

How about a brief history lesson? When our government was formed, a Constitution was written that described how our country's government would be formed. Included in the Constitution is a Bill of Rights, which lists the rights of all people who are citizens of our country. In the same way that our government gives privileges to all its citizens, you have the right to be treated with respect and dignity by those who make up your family and circle of friends and acquaintances. (How's that for tying together history and your life? Who said history is a boring subject?)

Unfortunately, not all teenagers are treated with the dignity they deserve. When children grow older, they often stand up for themselves and assert their rights, especially if they believe that their personal rights have been squashed for too long. While this can be a healthy exercise, young people who believe their rights have been denied can become rebellious. They may say things such as:

"I'm tired of being treated like dirt!"

"I'm sick of talking to people who refuse to listen."

"I don't feel like cooperating—I'm going to do things my way from now on!"

"Who cares what your opinion is? Your opinion doesn't matter anymore."

They may do things such as:

★ Deliberately violate rules, even rules that are meant to help

★ Encourage their peers to join them in rebelling

★ Dress or act in ways they know will irritate others

★ Give up on themselves

Rebellion is a communication device that hurt young people use to say, "I think my rights as a person are being violated. I want to be taken seriously. I want others to treat me the way I deserve to be treated." The message of rebellion often needs to be heard! However, the voice of rebellion can be clouded by such strong anger that its message is lost. Worse, it can keep a teenager stuck in a vicious cycle of fights and arguments and poor choices that can ultimately destroy her relationships and even her self-esteem.

All teens have rights—including you. You have the right to be happy, to say "no" to someone who mistreats you, to make your own decisions, to be whatever you want to be as a person. Learning to properly stand up for your rights will go a long way toward convincing others to make sure that your rights are protected.

Sound Off

What are some common ways teenagers rebel in order to have their rights met?

_____

_____

_____

_____

When teenagers rebel, how do others respond to them?

_____

_____

_____

_____

In what ways is rebellion effective? Ineffective?

EFFECTIVE	INEFFECTIVE
1.	1.
2.	2.
3.	3.
4.	4.
5.	5.

What personal rights are unmet in your life?

_____

_____

_____

What are some healthy ways you can influence others to respect your rights?

_____

_____

_____

Assignment

Make a list of your Top Ten Personal Rights and share it with a trusted friend.

_____   _____

_____   _____

_____   _____

_____   _____

_____   _____

Think About It! Is it wrong to rebel? No, not really. The risk of rebellion is that if you do it frequently or with great force, no one will take you seriously. People will simply roll their eyes and say to themselves, "There she goes again." Change never happens unless a person says to herself and others, "Things will be different in me, starting right now." The words you choose, behaviors you display, and actions you take make all the difference in whether others take you seriously. Should you rebel against mistreatment? Yes, but rebel gracefully.

Useful Tip

Make a habit of asking what happens after you rebel. If rebellion is positive, change should take place. If rebellion results in greater understanding, fewer fights, honest communication or clearing the air, it was good. If rebellion results in misunderstanding, more fights, verbal brawls, or hostile feelings, it was probably ill-advised.

Voices of Victory

Me, I was a fighter, man. I was good at it, too. If someone made me mad, I decked them. But after a while, fighting is no good. You got no friends. No one respects you. You're in trouble all the time. I finally decided that I was going to learn to fight smart. Now I don't argue just because I feel like it. I only argue when it's the only right thing to do.

—Tory, age 16

Feeling Close to People

Relationships are one of the most vital parts of life. Without them we could not function. Depending on your childhood experiences, you may or may not have good relationships. Perhaps you have trouble making and keeping friends. Or maybe you make friends easily, but too often people run over you or your friendships seem to fall apart.

If you took a poll of the general public and asked them to name the things that get in the way of solid, lasting relationships, here are some of the traits they would probably name:

- Talking too much

- Not talking enough

- Clinging to others; smothering them

- Taking control of conversations

- Quickly expressing your opinion, even if no one wants to know it

- Telling lies

- Gossiping about other people

- Breaking another person's confidence

- Negative remarks; cutting language

- Placing all the blame on others

- Not listening

- Frequent cursing

Do any of these sound familiar? Troubled young people frequently complain about unsatisfactory relationships. The good news is that all healthy relationships should be 50/50. Each person brings an equal amount to a friendship. That means that you have a considerable influence in the development of new relationships.

Maybe you have been so badly hurt in previous relationships that it is hard for you to trust others. You want to have more and better friendships but you lack confidence—in yourself and in others.

Social skills can be learned. If you feel you will never be good at forming lasting relationships, perhaps what you need is practice at saying and doing the things that attract others to you. Change won't happen overnight, but if you keep working at it, people will notice—and they will be attracted to you.

Dig Deep

What are some of your social strengths?

1.

2.

3.

What are some of your social weaknesses?

1.

2.

3.

How would you help a person who is shy and has trouble approaching a potential new friend?

_____

_____

_____

How can she help herself?

_____

_____

_____

How would you help a person who is loud and negative and curses a lot?

_____

_____

_____

How can she help herself?

_____

_____

_____

Assignment

Make a promise to reach out to someone who needs a new friend (and then do it). Make another promise to try to improve at least one of your social weaknesses.

Think About It! You define yourself by passing judgment on your strengths and weaknesses. But it's hard to accurately decide what you are good at and where your weaknesses lie. People frequently overestimate their weaknesses and downplay their strengths, or vice versa. An important task of recovery is to constantly question yourself: Are you where you want to be? Are there things you can do (or avoid doing) to get along better with others? Work toward getting where you want to be in relationships and being who you want to be socially. Relating to others improves as you relate honestly with yourself.

Behavior Watch: Immature Love

The experience of sexual abuse can cause a survivor to ask, *What is love?* Seems like a simple question, but it's not. When one person helps another person grow emotionally, socially, or even spiritually, that's an expression of love. Of course, there's the kind of love that involves sexual feelings. Even in romantic relationships, love is an emotion that helps people grow. Watch out if these signs are present in your relationships (romantic or otherwise). If they are, love may be immature or absent altogether.

- You seem to care about the other person more than he cares about you.
- The same problems keep coming up—and never get solved.
- Jealousy is involved.
- Control is involved.
- You are expected to say things, do things, or dress in a way that's not "you."
- You are expected to change, but the other person isn't.
- No room for other relationships is allowed.
- When the emotion wears off, the other person looks awfully dull.

——Live What You Believe——

Read each of the following statements and rate how strongly you agree with that statement on a scale of 1 (strongly disagree) to 10 (strongly agree):

- ⬦ Divorce is sometimes a good thing.

- ⬦ Teenagers and adults should not experiment with drugs or alcohol.

- ⬦ Sex should be saved for marriage.

- ⬦ A good education is the best way to get ahead in life.

- ⬦ Adults should not spank their children.

Have you ever been with a group of friends when a "hot" topic—like those listed above—comes up? Your friends are likely to express their opinions on the issue, sometimes quite forcefully. We all have beliefs and opinions. Some we feel more strongly than others. For example, you may strongly believe that adults should not spank their children. So if an adult mistreated you or a friend, you might feel very hurt or angry.

Opinions and beliefs vary greatly from one teenager to another. Experts say that one of the best ways to determine the strength of a person's beliefs is to observe the way they act. The stronger the belief, the greater the reaction.

Trouble arises when a young person's behavior *does not* match her beliefs. For the young person who believes that adults should not mistreat children, but says and does nothing after being abused, guilt and shame may emerge. Or, a young person may swear that she will never get drunk again, but in a moment of weakness, she gives in to pressure and does the very thing she said she would never do.

Guilt can actually be a positive emotion. It may push you to examine what you believe and cause you to try to match that belief in your behavior. There may be good reasons why your behavior and beliefs do not match up. Perhaps you were afraid of what someone might say or do. Embarrassment or uncertainty can keep you from acting on your opinions. Whatever the reason, it is healthy to take a look at what you believe and see how closely it matches how you behave.

As you understand why you believe what you do, you will be able to relate to others better. You will be able to understand why they are the way they are. Understanding of others is the first step in tolerating differences.

What's Your Perspective?

Imagine that the target on the right represents the things you believe and value. How closely does your behavior match your beliefs? Do you hit the bull's-eye or miss the target altogether? Ask a friend if she thinks your behavior "hits the mark" when compared to what you claim to believe.

Suppose you believe that something is wrong (like abusing drugs or alcohol) and yet you do it anyway . . .

How do you feel about your choice?

_____

_____

_____

_____

What makes you choose to do something that goes against your opinions and beliefs?

_____

_____

_____

_____

Read the following scenario and answer the questions:

> *Sherri was abused by lots of people as a child—her mother, mother's boyfriend, a cousin. The list was a long one. Because of her childhood experiences, she developed a strong opinion that people should be treated with respect. She constantly demanded that she be treated the way any person would want to be treated. Yet, whenever a new person moved to her school, she made a point of putting that person "in her place." When her friends pointed out that her behavior did not match what she claimed to believe, Sherri became angry.*

What is your opinion of Sherri? Are there any reasons or excuses for her behavior?

_____

_____

_____

What advice would you give to Sherri?

_____

_____

_____

What would keep her from accepting your advice and doing as you suggest?

_____

_____

_____

Think About It!

It's one thing to know what you believe. You have opinions just like everyone else. You may even know where your opinions came from—your strong-willed mother, your meek father, a competitive sibling. Tracing your opinions to their origin is not as hard as learning to think and relate differently. Thinking in new ways means opening yourself to change, questioning old habits, and finding different strategies. Learn to "scan" your body. Take note of how you feel physically and emotionally in every situation. What you notice about yourself can give a hint at the changes you need to make. Be bold and try out new behaviors.

Useful Tip

Be aware of the thoughts connected to your guilty feelings. Also be aware that these thoughts may not be accurate. You might believe that you are helpless when the opposite is actually true. Be brave enough to ask, "Am I really that bad or do I just think I am?" There are two lines from a famous poem that say: *I am the master of my fate;/I am the captain of my soul.* In the long run, you are the one who decides what kind of person you will be. Think positively!

Voices of Victory

I tried to forgive my stepbrother for abusing me. It didn't work. Know why? I couldn't forgive myself. Before I could move on with my life I had to learn to be good to myself. And that means forgiveness. Believe me, it isn't easy, but once I forgave myself for things that I did (and for some things I didn't even do but felt guilty about anyway), I could forgive other people.

—Annie, age 16

Whom Can You Trust?

In the 1960s a popular phrase was "Never trust anyone over thirty." It's hard enough for any young person to know whom to trust, but for those who have endured trauma, trust becomes a slippery word indeed. About the best any trauma survivor can say is that some people can be trusted and others cannot. Problem is, how do you know who belongs in which group?

Abusive events may cause you to question seemingly everything and everyone. You may ask yourself an unending string of questions:

"What do people have against me?"

"If I tell him what I think, how will he use it to manipulate me?"

"Should I share my feelings or keep them to myself?"

"Am I all alone in the way I feel?"

"How will I make it in life if I can't count on people to help me?"

"Is there any use in trusting anyone?"

Healthy trust in others is the beginning of meaningful relationships. But once a young person has been violated in any way, she may approach all new relationships by thinking back on the past:

"Does this person truly understand me?"

"Is her show of concern sincere?"

"Am I ready to make a commitment to becoming close to him?"

"Will I be hurt one more time?"

"When should I reveal what's really going on inside me?"

"Am I better off being around people or being alone?"

Mistrust occurs when your needs are not met. Entering relationships based on mutual trust can create for you a new world of confidence. You can . . .

★ Act with confidence that you can make right choices

★ Speak with confidence that you will be understood

★ Relate to others with confidence that they truly care about you

★ Love yourself with confidence that you are worth loving

★ Give to others with confidence that you can make a difference in this world

What Do You Think?

Take yourself back to the 1960s and rewrite that popular slogan "Never trust anyone over thirty."

Never trust anyone . . .

_____

_____

_____

Think of some of the people you trust and ask why you can trust those people.

Person I trust   **Reason I trust that person**

_____   _____

_____   _____

_____   _____

Now think of the people you cannot trust and ask yourself why you cannot trust them.

Person I do not trust   **Reason I do not trust that person**

_____   _____

_____   _____

_____   _____

Be honest with yourself:

Yes	No	I am too quick to judge or mistrust others.
Yes	No	I have difficulty trusting any person who is the same sex as the person who violated me.
Yes	No	I think I can learn to trust others again.
Yes	No	Because of trust issues, I keep my distance from others.
Yes	No	Because of my need to be wanted, I am too quick to trust others.

Finish the following sentence:
One way I can build better trust in myself and others is . . .

_____

_____

_____

Think About It!
Virtually no one enters a new relationship and immediately decides to completely trust the person they've just met. It's normal to gradually show bits and pieces of your thoughts and emotions. As time passes, you can determine if a person is trustworthy. People who can be trusted share several key qualities. Even though you and she may be different, she does not act like something she is not. She enjoys you despite your flaws and weaknesses. She listens and seems to understand you as well as she does herself. She enters your world and receives you just as you are. Trustworthy people cause you to feel completely free to be you.

Useful Tip

It's too much to ask an abuse survivor to immediately trust others. The sad truth is that not all people can or should be trusted. On the flip side, many people are trustworthy and should not be shut out. Follow these guidelines as you learn to trust people:

- Don't ask for more than the other person can give.
- Be clear when you let people know what you need from them.
- Listen to your "gut feelings."
- Go slow. Time will help you know whom to trust.
- Rather than be bitter about the past, learn from it.

Trust is something you just do. It's actually a skill you can develop. Trust comes when you let life be your teacher.

Voices of Victory

Where am I? Do I love myself? Hate myself? Have I learned nothing? Have I learned a lot? Am I stuck in the past? Looking to the future? Am I powerful? Am I weak? Do I take care of myself? Am I ruining everything I have to live for? Who do I believe? Them? Me? Where am I?

—Michelle, age 15

The Art of Listening

Experts tell us that only a small percentage of communication is verbal. Up to 90 percent of communication is through gestures, tone of voice, facial expressions, even eye movement. Young people who are stuck in unhealthy relationships often complain that their communication with others isn't what they want it to be. They feel misunderstood. They don't understand others. Too often they find themselves in dead-end conversations.

Most young people assume that good communicators have a great vocabulary, or know when to say the right thing, or are persuasive. While these are great communication tools, they are not as important as the ability to *listen*. Listening involves more than hearing what another person has to say. Listening involves . . .

- Paying close attention to "body language"

- Thinking the way the other person thinks

- Being open to different opinions or points of view

- Picturing yourself "walking in someone else's shoes"

- Asking questions so you can have a deeper understanding

Take note the next time you are with a group of people. Some will dominate the conversation. Others will forcefully state their opinions. A few will fall for whatever everyone else says. Though it may not be evident immediately, the strongest group member is the one who listens to the others. Should you take a vote of who is the most influential group member, most likely it will be the one who listens best, not those who speak the loudest or talk the fastest.

Relationships are built on communication. And communication begins with the ability to listen. People who have learned to listen report . . .

- ★ A deeper appreciation for others

- ★ Greater satisfaction in conversations

- ★ Feeling respected by others

- ★ Higher self-esteem

- ★ Stronger tolerance for those who are different

- ★ Friendships that last

- ★ A stronger ability to work through personal problems

Relationships take on greater depth when partners can dig deeply into one another's feelings and understand each other's true thoughts and emotions. Not only will you feel more positively about yourself, but you will be a help to others, too.

Practice What You've Learned

Consider the following scenario and try to "listen" for the underlying message.

A teenager has just learned that she is pregnant. She fears that her family will not be supportive of her. She has no one else to turn to, so she comes to you. She explains, "My parents have told me not to be with my boyfriend, but he's the only one who loves me. I don't like that I'm pregnant, but even worse, I dread having to tell my family because I know they will be mad at me."

What emotions does this girl feel?

_____

_____

_____

What could you say to show her you understand what she feels?

_____

_____

_____

_____

What should you *avoid* saying to this girl?

_____

_____

_____

_____

Name some ways your relationships will improve as you try to become a better listener.

1.

2.

3.

4.

Think About It! Every person benefits when listening takes place. It feels good to be on the receiving end. It also feels good to be on the giving end of listening. When you listen, truly listen, to someone, you find yourself magically drifting into her world. You know her thoughts, feel her emotions, and guess what it must be like to be her. Listening does not mean sitting quietly until a person finishes speaking. Listening is hard work—as hard as anything you will ever do. The end result, though, is a capacity to connect to people in a way that you've never before experienced!

Behavior Watch: Communication Killers

It's no secret that good relationships involve healthy communication. Communication is not something that just happens among people. It's something we do. Communication is a skill, and good communication can be learned. Teens who communicate well with others avoid these mistakes:

- Talking so much that no one can get a word in edgewise

- Talking so little that people wonder if you have a pulse

- Complaining that "You don't understand me"

- Giving your opinions so often that everyone knows them all by heart

- Speaking before the other person finishes his sentence

- Teasing, taunting, or making fun of others

- Spreading secrets, lies, opinions, or gossip about people

Teenagers are attracted to other teenagers who have good communication skills. Your ability to make lasting friendships often depends on how well you interact with others.

Useful Tip

"Active listening" is a term used by communication experts. In its most basic form, active listening calls for you (the listener) to show the speaker that you are listening by paraphrasing what she has just said. She says, "I'm sick of the way people treat me." You might say, "You want to be treated like a real person." Active listening is proof positive that you have entered the other person's world and are truly trying to see life as she does.

Being Honest

Fear is a powerful emotion—so powerful that it can grip you and refuse to let you go. As a trauma survivor, it's likely you feel emotionally crippled. For that reason, you may choose to hide from others the way you truly feel. And even when you do share yourself openly with others, you do it with great care and uneasiness. Too often the emotional displays of trauma victims are shallow or explosive. Through extreme forms of communication you are making a statement, but it's not an honest expression of how you really feel. Consider the following examples of emotional dishonesty:

Alton is emotionally withdrawn. He keeps to himself and hardly ever interacts with his peers. When he is around people, he seldom looks them squarely in the eye. If his opinion is asked, he says what he thinks others want to hear.

Desired communication: I feel lonely. I'm unsure that anyone can understand my pain, but I wish I could share it with someone. I'm not important, so I doubt that anyone wants to get close to me.

What others might think: He's nobody. You try to talk to him, but he won't let you be friendly to him. He probably doesn't want to get better.

Sherika tells everyone exactly what she thinks. She voices what she likes about others, what she dislikes, where they can get off. She seldom thinks a thought that she does not express. Even when people don't care about her opinion, she gives it. She's quick to put people down with sharp comments.

Desired communication: I want to be liked, but I'm afraid that if I don't speak up, I won't get any attention. I hate coming across as being angry, but whatever is necessary to be taken seriously, I'll do it.

What others might think: She's rude. She's so stuck on herself that she can't see things the way others do. She always insists on her way. Forget her. The only thing she causes is trouble.

The trouble with dishonest communication is that it keeps people from taking you seriously. Whether you understate or overstate what you feel, the message you want others to hear gets lost. Honest communication involves:

⋄ Saying what you feel in a composed and clear way

⋄ Choosing the right time and place to communicate what you feel

⋄ Doing all you can to make sure your words and actions match up

⋄ Refusing to use your words and actions to manipulate others

⋄ Listening to what others say to you and about you

Having Your Say

How can you tell when someone is being dishonest with themselves and others? What do they say and do?

Things Dishonest People Say

_____

_____

_____

_____

Things Dishonest People Do

_____

_____

_____

_____

How can you tell if someone is being honest with themselves and others? What do they say and do?

Things Honest People Say

_____

_____

_____

_____

Things Honest People Do

_____

_____

_____

_____

Some ways I can be more honest in my communication with others are:

1.

2.

3.

4.

5.

Assignment

The next time things seem to go wrong between you and someone else, take time to think about what you said and did. Be as candid with yourself as you can in discovering ways you failed to be honest with yourself and others. What did you learn?

Think About It!

Trauma survivors want to be themselves. It's no fun to be an "abuse victim." Victims find it hard to experience happiness. When you live the life of a victim, everything else seems unimportant. The fun parts of life become lost seas of tears and forests of darkness. Dishonesty sets in. Survivors are former victims who have learned to hope. Hope lifts the spirit. Hope gives the survivor something to work toward. Hope gives purpose. When a survivor hopes, she begins to believe that her current suffering will not last forever. With hope, the survivor can be honest with herself and others. Being "real" feels good again.

Voices of Victory

I thought that honest communication meant that I said exactly what I thought. I tried it and it didn't work. When I talked "honestly" with my friends, they stayed mad at me. Honest listening is when you say what you think, but you're still considerate of what your friend thinks, too.

—Elle, age 17

Power and Safety

Trauma survivors frequently report that they felt powerless after being abused. And why not? After all, sexual abuse represents one of the vilest ways one person forces power onto another. It makes sense, then, that the survivor would do what she can to recapture the feeling of personal power. When you feel power over yourself, you also feel safe.

"Power" is one of those words that can be positive or negative depending on its use. Power is positive if it allows you to have healthy control over your life so that you can be emotionally balanced and have meaningful relationships. Power is negative if it is used to overwhelm people. Negative power might give a temporary feeling of safety, but it destroys relationships, and ultimately it tears down self-esteem. Here are some common characteristics:

★ Taking on a "tough girl" attitude to shield against further pain

★ Evaluating others with anger, arrogance, or judgment

★ Suspiciously viewing the kindness and warmth of others as unnecessary

★ Acting like you know it all and don't need anyone's input

★ Showing a lack of interest in others

Like most exaggerated behaviors, negative power does more damage than good. Sure, in the short run it may keep you from being hurt again, but it also prevents you from receiving help. In the long run, displays of negative power do not keep you safe but cause you to get stuck in a hopeless world of loneliness and depression. Real power comes when you . . .

• Take time to observe yourself and admit to behaviors that tear down rather than build up

• Boldly state your case, but stay away from aggression

• Courageously explore your hurts and fears

• Make an effort to control yourself rather than others

• Accept the kindness and care of others

Survivors who refuse to push their anger and hurt onto others show real power. Power comes from personal control. And in *that* kind of power comes safety.

Your Reflections

In what way does your past abuse affect the way you trust others?

_____

_____

_____

On a scale of 1 to 10, are you too quick to trust people or too slow to trust?

1 _____ 10
too slow   too quick

What are some ways you try to have power over others?

1.

2.

3.

In what ways do "power struggles" cause you problems in relationships?

1.

2.

3.

What do you expect from relationships? Do you normally get what you expect? Explain.

_____

_____

_____

_____

Think About It! We live in a power-hungry world. It seems that we have been sold a bill of goods. All around us are messages that power is good. Power is desirable. People in power are important. But the kind of power that seems so popular in our society invites fear. Power is too often depicted as a muscular word. Power is really a tender word. Real power is shown when people step outside themselves and help others. Real power is shown when people set a good example. Real power is shown through compassion. A person who is at peace with herself is powerful indeed.

Behavior Watch: Taking Care of "Number One"

There comes a time when a teenager must be selfish. If your rights and needs have been violated, it's right and good to stand up for yourself and say, *I'm tired of being tromped on.* There are, of course, healthy and unhealthy ways to stand up for yourself. You are being appropriately selfish when you . . .

- Get out of a relationship that is not good for you, even if the other person protests

- Place limits on how you allow others to treat you or talk to you

- Say *no* to peers when you're not really interested in their suggestions

- Speak up when someone says or does something that makes you feel uncomfortable

- Demand more information before making a decision

Teenagers who are appropriately selfish are simply making sure that their rights and needs are being met. If your rights and needs are not met, the chances of personal improvement are slim. But once you have "filled your own bucket," not only will you flourish, you will have something to share with others.

Voices of Victory

I was really nervous the first time I talked with my therapist. I just knew she'd think I was a slut or a whore or something like that. But that's not how it was at all. I'll never forget how she soothed me and told me I was a good person. I felt safer than I had ever felt before. That's exactly what girls like me need—to feel safe.

—April, age 15

Friend or Foe?

All teenagers want friendships. And all teenagers want their friendships to benefit them. There's nothing better than having a friend who makes you feel important and helps you grow to be a better person. When friendships are real, that's what happens. On the flip side, there's not much that is more destructive than a relationship that harms you as a person. If a relationship keeps you from being a better person, you can bet that it's not real.

At first glance it seems that it is easy to tell the difference between a healthy friendship and a negative relationship. The truth is, it takes effort to determine which relationships should be continued and which ought to be tapered off. A relationship is usually healthy when . . .

⋄ Each friend shows consideration and courtesy to the other

⋄ Neither friend is controlling or domineering over the other

⋄ Both willingly listen to the other

⋄ Neither pressures the other to be something she is not

⋄ Similarities are enjoyed and differences are respected

⋄ Room is allowed for other friends and relationships

⋄ Disagreements are handled in a respectful manner

⋄ Both feel completely comfortable being themselves

⋄ Neither rushes to "fix" the other person's weaknesses

Teenagers who find themselves in negative relationships often have no idea how things turned sour. What started out seeming so right, turned out all wrong. To make things worse, too many teenagers go from one damaging relationship to another. It helps to know the warning signs of a relationship that needs to be avoided or even ended. They include . . .

★ One teenager seems to dominate and control the other

★ Too much emphasis is given to outward appearance rather than inner beauty

★ One or both seems more interested in what he/she gets than what he/she gives

★ Frequent arguments become intense and are often unresolved

★ Jealousy blossoms when others try to befriend you

★ One demands that the other be just like he/she wants her to be

★ Heavy demands are placed on your time and energy

★ You are pressured to do things you probably would not do on your own

★ Instead of support and encouragement, you receive advice and criticism

The friendships you form during your teenage years are often more important than family relationships in determining how you think and feel about yourself. Teenagers tend to look to one another for help as much or more than they do family members or other adults. Rather than walk into friendships blindly, be aware of how they can help or hurt you as you continue to grow to be a better person.

It's Your Turn

When you meet someone for the first time, what qualities do you normally pay attention to most?

I pay attention to . . .   **Because . . .**

_____   _____

_____   _____

_____   _____

_____   _____

The people I feel closest to help me become a better person by . . .

_____

_____

_____

_____

I have to admit that I've been in relationships that hurt me more than they helped me. I know that because . . .

_____

_____

Whenever I enter a new relationship, I plan to . . .

_____

_____

_____

_____

Think About It!
It's much easier to walk into negative relationships than it is to build healthy friendships. Put bluntly, it's easier to make enemies than it is to make friends. Forging friendships requires work and time. Making friends is something you *do.* Too often we talk about becoming friends when it is more accurate to say that friendships are made. What's more, the building of friendships is pleasant work. You will never find anything more satisfying than making a friend.

Voices of Victory

I went for years without a true friend. Part of the reason was because I doubted that anyone wanted to be my friend. Why would any teenager in her right mind want to be friends with a girl who had been having sex since she was seven years old? I did all the wrong things. I told lies about people, put them down, treated them rude. And then I was dumb enough to complain about not having any friends. Duh! About two years ago it finally hit me that the reason I didn't have any friends was me! I had gone so long pushing people away from me that it was hard to start being nice. It felt weird being polite and all that. But it worked. I'm not saying that I'm anywhere close to being perfect. But I have several really good friends now.

—Ashley, age 14

Latching On

All people are social creatures. No one lives in a completely isolated world. Ours is a world full of people who are connected to one another in many different ways. We all take note of the way those around us act. When you hear a friend state an opinion, you compare her thoughts to your own. When you see a person react to a situation, you ask yourself if you would have acted the same way. When a peer cries or laughs or screams, you find yourself thinking of how you might have handled the situation.

Whether or not you realize it, you constantly evaluate what you see in others. Sometimes you think to yourself, "I disagree with him." Or perhaps you think, "I would have done things differently." Or maybe you think, "I agree 100 percent with what she just said." In many ways you live through the actions and statements of others. That is, you identify with other people even though you may not be completely aware of it. Quite often you receive satisfaction when you see someone do or say things you would like to say or do. You live, so to speak, through that person.

You can discover valuable lessons about yourself by taking note of the people you are attracted to. You are making a statement about yourself in the relations you keep. Consider the following examples . . .

★ *Karen hangs around boys who are in a gang. They talk tough and sometimes fight their rivals. Karen never fights and even encourages the boys to be good. But when they do the things gang members do, she silently enjoys their aggression. She wishes she had the guts to stand up to people like they do. By associating with gang members, Karen is living out her violent and aggressive feelings.*

★ *A group of girls has a bad reputation among the "preps." The preps accuse these girls of having loose morals. They say that the girls "do it" with boys all the time. They whisper when anyone in this group smokes cigarettes or drinks beer, as if they're any better. For some reason April is attracted to the "bad" girls rather than the "good" kids. Even though she doesn't mess around with boys and has never smoked a cigarette or guzzled beer, she likes the fact that the bad girls are bold enough to rebel. The way April sees things, it's the "do-gooders" who cause problems. After all, the cousin who sexually abused her was a prep just like them.*

Who you side with says a lot about who you are. All teenagers want to be a part of a group, but even more than that, all teenagers want to be a part of a group that seems to think and feel the way they do. There's nothing wrong with group involvement. Belonging to a group is a basic human need. Be aware, though, that the groups you choose reflect something about who you are.

Sound Off

React to the following statements:

When I see someone who is real popular, I think . . .

_____

_____

_____

When I hear the thoughts of someone who has an opinion about everything, I think . . .

_____

_____

_____

When I'm around people who do wild and crazy things "just because," I think . . .

_____

_____

_____

When I watch a movie, I identify with the good guy/the bad guy (pick one) because . . .

_____

_____

_____

Many abuse survivors feel emotions that they simply cannot talk about. What are some of the emotions you have difficulty expressing?

_____

_____

_____

Name the types of people you like to associate with. What is it about those people that attracts you?

Kind of Person   **Attracts Me Because . . .**

_____   _____

_____   _____

_____   _____

What statement are you making when you identify with these different types of people?

_____

_____

_____

_____

Think About It! Sometimes it's easy to say what you think. Other times, you wish others could speak for you. Often, teenagers join a group because they want to send a message to others. There's nothing wrong with that. Everyone needs to belong. Be honest with yourself, though, when you choose your friends. Ask yourself if the statement you are making by hanging out with the people you do is helping you or hurting you. Be bold enough to make good choices in your peer group. Make a positive statement.

Behavior Watch: Relationship Boundaries

When you were abused, someone crossed an important boundary, one that should not have been violated. It seems that it should not be so hard to put boundaries on relationships—but it is, especially with the opposite sex. Stay away from relationships if:

- You have to ask the other person, "Do you really love me?"

- One or both of you keeps major secrets from the other

- You are in the relationship just to get away from another boyfriend, or from your family

- Sex is the main thing that attracts you to one another

- You have to convince yourself that he will eventually change for the better (he probably won't)

- One of you avoids small talk and goes straight for sex

- You have frequent fights followed by lavish making up

- He gets angry over little things

- You're the one who pays the consequences for the things you do

Voices of Victory

Don't even talk to me about being wild. Wild girls complain about the "preps" and talk bad about the popular kids. Want to know my opinion? I think the wild teenagers just wish they were popular, but they're not, so they go crazy. It's called pretending to be someone you're not. I know, I've been there, done that.

—Jodi, age 18

═══Tell It All═══

When you feel an emotion you can do several things with it:

★ Keep it to yourself

★ Let someone else know how you feel

★ Turn it on yourself

★ Turn it on someone else

After going through abuse, you cannot help but have an emotional reaction. It's going to happen. (You already know that.) What you do with those emotions not only affects how you feel about yourself, but how you relate to others. Consider the following:

• If you keep your feelings to yourself, you will feel that no one understands you. You will believe that people cannot relate to you. How can they? They don't know what's going on inside you! All others can do is guess what you're experiencing.

• Letting others know how you feel may put you in an awkward position. What if they don't understand? What if they say or do things that make your situation worse? Or what if you reveal your feelings and then feel humiliated, as if you have now let the whole world know that something is terribly wrong with you? Of course, telling someone about your feelings might help. Maybe, just maybe, the other person will understand and help you.

• Turning your feelings on yourself usually results in one of two conditions (and maybe both): depression and anxiety. Abuse survivors frequently talk about wanting to punish themselves, feeling urges to self-abuse, and hating life so much that dying seems better than living. Obviously, none of these alternatives does much to improve relations with others.

• If you turn your emotions on others, you might feel relieved because you've unloaded personal stress, but in the process you have also failed to win friends and influence people. Abuse victims who unload on others predictably find themselves running into trouble with authority figures—and no one wants to bail them out.

In order for you to relate to others in ways that help rather than hurt, you must be completely comfortable with your feelings. You were abused and you are angry. It hurts to go through the humiliation you feel. You want revenge on the person who mistreated you. It's okay to feel those things. Acceptance of your emotions sets you up for relationships that ultimately benefit you.

Dig Deep

Rate yourself on a scale of 1 to 10 on the following statements:

I keep my feelings (especially about my abuse) to myself.

1 _____ 10
unlike me   like me

I tell others how I feel.

1 _____ 10
unlike me   like me

I turn my feelings on myself.

1 _____ 10
unlike me   like me

I turn my feelings on others.

1 _____ 10
unlike me   like me

If I tell others exactly what I think, they are likely to believe this about me:

_____

_____

_____

_____

Revealing my true feelings to others might hurt me because . . .

_____

_____

_____

Revealing my true feelings to others might help me because . . .

_____

_____

_____

Think About It! The most important thing you can do is tell yourself how you feel about your abuse experience. When you are honest with yourself, you are then free to be honest with others. Telling it all to others does not mean you must tell everybody everything about you. Over time, you will discover which adults and friends you can trust. You should feel free to build healthy relationships with those people. But to relate effectively with others, you must first be honest (tell it all) with yourself.

Useful Tip

Trouble getting along with other teenagers? Adults? It's common for teenagers to complain about not being able to get along with certain people. Most often—it seems—teens wish the other person would change. How many times have you heard a teenager say, "If he'd treat me better, we'd get along just fine" or "Why does she make so many rules?" or "I try as hard as I can to help her, but she won't listen." Maybe you feel that you've been the victim of bad relationships for too many years. If so, there are a few things you can do:

- Check your own attitude at the door. He may have a bad attitude, but things get worse if your attitude matches his.

- Stand up for yourself in the right way. No need to drag everybody down to your level, but there's also no need to be everyone's punching bag.

- Refuse to get caught in a war of words. When a fight starts, be brave and step away.

- Say what you mean and mean what you say. But be nice at the same time.

- Don't assume that everyone thinks the same as you. Leave room for disagreement.

Let Your Secrets Out

You've heard that old saying, "It takes two to tango." For those of you who've never heard of it, the tango is a dance that went out of style long ago. Somehow sayings often linger even as social customs change. Oh well, that's progress. What this old adage suggests is that the successes and failures of a relationship depend on the behaviors of both people—you and the other person.

Here's something to think about. In every relationship, *you* decide how much of your true self you will reveal. In some relationships, you feel comfortable enough to tell the other person almost everything about yourself. With other people, you reveal virtually nothing. It takes very little to guess which relationships tend to be the most satisfying. When you are true to yourself and others, your relationships benefit.

Trauma survivors often report that they have trouble trusting others. Even though they want healthy relations with friends or family members, they may keep things to themselves "just to be safe." There's nothing wrong with being safe in a relationship. That's smart.

But there comes a time when something gets in the way of a potentially healthy relationship. Pride can keep a teenager from building the support she needs from family and friends. Here's how pride damages an abuse survivor's relationships:

⬦ Something happened in the past that hurt you. It hurt when it happened and it still hurts when you think about it in the present.

⬦ Even if only a few people know about it, *you* know that you are in emotional pain. You feel that pain each and every day.

⬦ Rather than let others know that you are struggling with any issues, you keep your thoughts to yourself. Pride refuses to let you show that you have any weaknesses.

⬦ By being what you think others want you to be rather than being who you are—flaws and all—the relationship suffers. You spend as much (or more) effort keeping secrets as you do making the relationship work.

You have no control over what others bring into a relationship with you. Chances are pretty good that your friend or family member has hidden emotional aches and pains, too. As you shed your emotional pride, you bring a genuine quality to the relationship. You can't control how others act around you, but by dropping your pride and being "all you," your influence on the relationship is healthy. Chances that the relationship will also be healthy are improved.

Be Honest with Yourself

Read the following statements and pick the one that is most like you:

1. When I enter a relationship, I'm quick to tell the other person all about myself.

2. When I enter a relationship, I wait a long time to tell the other person all about myself.

3. When I enter a relationship, chances are good that I will never tell the other person all about myself.

4. When I enter a relationship, I will probably tell lies about who I really am.

The reason I chose the statement above is . . .

_____

_____

_____

Pride can make me a *better* person because when I am proud of myself I . . .

_____

_____

_____

_____

Pride can *hurt* my relationships because when I have too much pride I . . .

_____

_____

_____

_____

Assignment

Make an effort to let go of your pride over the next few days. Be appropriately open with others. Notice the change it makes in your relationships.

Think About It! It's never too late to examine your relationships. In fact, the teenage years are a great time to examine relationships. Ask yourself how you can be more open and honest with others. Become aware of the secrets you keep from people. As you learn to share the full range of your thoughts and feelings with your friends and family, you are taking healthy steps toward strengthening relationship ties.

Behavior Watch: The Perfectionist

Pride can push a teenager to insist on perfection. Too stiff to loosen up and be herself, the prideful teen finds herself inching toward rigid perfection. Here are some traits of the perfectionist. If you see these qualities in yourself, take note of them and try to let go of the pride that pushes you in that direction:

- Keeps her thoughts and feelings tightly to herself
- Seems to expect the worst to happen—and it does
- Stingy in giving, stingy with emotions
- Expects too much from self and from others
- Hides a weak self-esteem behind a mask of supposed strength
- Won't admit to wrongdoing

Voices of Victory

What's wrong with me? Why do I cry over everything? Why does everything bother me? Why can't I accept a compliment? Why can't I give compliments? Am I that stubborn? Am I that proud? Am I really afraid? I think so.

—Tonya, age 17

Getting Better

The Magic of "Love"

The word "love" may be one of the most misunderstood words in the English language. We all think we know what it's supposed to be, but our experiences may have caused us to believe that love isn't all that great.

Depending on where you learned about love, you may have been led to believe that love is . . .

★ Giving in to sexual pressure

★ Mountains of mushy feelings

★ "Owning" another person

★ Something everybody does by the time they become teenagers

★ Being attached to something or someone

★ A "high" feeling that never goes away

★ Something people daydream about, but it's not real

True love is more than all that. It is both wonderful and complicated. Sometimes love does involve sex. Sometimes it gives you goose bumps. When two people love one other, they may never want to let go of each another. Love can cause an emotional high so great, it's intoxicating! But when young people are abused, they may leave the experience thinking that they will never know real love. Fortunately, all people are capable of knowing and feeling love. It's a universal emotion.

There is a simple test you can use to determine if the feeling inside you is true love: *Love is an emotion that causes you or someone else to grow into a better person.*

While that simple rule provides the best guideline for knowing if you are experiencing love, there are a few more things to know about this emotion.

◇ When you give love away, it comes back to you if it is real.

◇ To truly love someone else, you must first love yourself. If you do not, then whatever you are feeling is not really love.

◇ For love to survive, you must work to make it last. Love is not only a feeling, but a commitment to someone or something great.

◇ If you think you have loved someone, but you were hurt in the experience, what you felt may not have been love. Even when a truly loving experience is over, you will be a better person.

◇ Love and sex are two different things. True love can involve sex, but sex does not require love. If someone has hurt you sexually, love was not involved.

◇ Just because "everybody is doing it" does not mean that what they are doing involves love. "Doing it" usually involves things like lust, or possessiveness, or jealousy, or even power.

◇ If you feel fear, you are not experiencing love. Love and fear do not mix.

What's Your Perspective?

Below are listed some sources where young people get information about love. Number in order the three sources that provided you the most information about love:

Friends ____	Family ____	Other adult ____
Magazines ____	Movies ____	School ____
Church ____	Experience ____	Doctor ____

What were the messages you learned about love from these sources?

_____

_____

_____

What is the difference in the words "lust," "sex," and "love"?

Lust is _____

Sex is _____

Love is _____

Does a person who abuses children know the meaning of the word "love"? Explain.

_____

_____

_____

_____

_____

How does sexual abuse get in the way of a victim's understanding of the word "love"?

_____

_____

_____

If you could tell someone a positive lesson you have learned about love, what would it be?

_____

_____

_____

_____

Think About It! Love may be one of the most misunderstood of all emotions. We all say that we know what it means to love and be loved, but the truth is that love is so deep, so broad, so complex, so puzzling that no one fully understands it. It's the greatness of love that makes it such a desirable emotion. We all want it even though none of us can adequately define it. Perhaps it's the mystery of love that pulls us toward it like a magnet attracts metal objects.

Useful Tip

If love is an emotion that causes you or another person to grow, it must be complicated (and it is). Some people say teenagers aren't mature enough to love, *really* love someone. Maybe adults aren't either. Love is hard work. The seeds you sow now in learning what love is will pay off in your adult years. You may never know all that love involves, but you certainly won't be hurt by trying to find out.

Voices of Victory

I thought I knew what love is. Then I started to really think about it. Man is it ever a complicated emotion. I know this: Love is way more than that sexy feeling you get when you're attracted to someone. I think you know what I mean. Yeah, love's more than that. It's a cool feeling. I'm going to find out all I can about love. Then I'm going to live it. I can't wait.

—Robin, age 16

Easing the Pain

Pain is one of those words with multiple layers of meaning. You can experience pain when . . .

- ◇ You cut your finger

- ◇ You get a shot

- ◇ You hear your parents fight and argue

- ◇ You are mistreated or abused

Pain can be as minor as a scratch on your body or as major as a gaping wound to your heart. For centuries people have tried to understand why we experience pain. Some say it's because people are bad by nature. Others say it's simply because people can make choices that hurt. Whatever the reason, pain is a part of our world—and we all know what it means.

One of the greatest insights a person can ever receive is that pain can actually make a person better. Think about it:

- • Pain can warn a person to stay away from potential harm.

- • Pain motivates a person to look for a way out of a bad situation.

- • Pain causes people to appreciate the little things in life that are good.

- • Pain allows one person to understand a friend's troubles.

- • Pain can force a person to take time to heal.

Of course, too much pain can pull you into depression or fear or mistrust. Repeated abuse can make you angry, bitter, or frightened. If pain is not confronted, it can paralyze you. But when you figure out how to use pain as a chance to learn about yourself and others, growth accelerates at a rapid pace.

There are no simple answers for dealing with the pain in your life, but here are some guidelines that have helped people move beyond their painful past:

- ★ People make choices, and sometimes those choices are downright bad. But one person's poor choice does not mean that the victim is a bad person. All people have the capacity to be good (and that includes you).

- ★ Every single day, you have the opportunity to make choices. By learning to make good ones, you can make up for some of the mistakes from your past.

- ★ Pain can be a wake-up call that makes us appreciate the small favors others do for us.

- ★ Because you have survived pain, you are capable of understanding another person's experience. When you extend a helping hand to that person, both of you feel better.

- ★ Once you allow yourself to express your feelings openly, you open yourself up to receive the kindness that supportive friends are ready to give you.

Having Your Say

What is the worst kind of pain you can imagine? What is it that makes that pain so bad?

_____

_____

_____

_____

_____

_____

_____

If a person feels emotional pain because she has been abused or mistreated, it means (choose one):

    a. The abuser gave her what she deserved.

    b. The abuser made a terrible choice and she is suffering the consequences.

    c. Life is fair and she had it coming to her.

    d. All people should not be trusted.

What are some loving ways to respond to a person who is in pain?

    1.

    2.

    3.

    4.

    5.

Name at least one positive thing that has happened to you because you have experienced pain:

_____

_____

Finish this sentence:
    I plan to ease my pain by . . .

_____

_____

Think About It! Life hurts. There's no way to avoid that reality. For as long as people have wondered why we suffer pain, no one has found an easy explanation. The story of pain is a story that every person can tell. As you tell your story, listen. Listen for opportunities to choose. Listen for opportunities to love. Listen for opportunities to change. Listen for opportunities to make a better world for yourself. Pain will not leave you. But pain does not need to wreck you. Pain pushes you to find a new way. You can give in to suffering, or you can choose personal freedom. Choose to be free to love yourself in spite of your discomfort.

Behavior Watch: Depression

Too often we think of depression as something that happens to us. Depression, it seems, cannot be avoided. Sure, depression can do a number on its victim, but the victim can also do something about depression. You can help yourself overcome depression by doing the following:

- Acknowledge to yourself and others that you are unhappy. You might like to make a list of the things or circumstances that cause you dissatisfaction.

- Do a personal search of the ways you talk negatively to yourself or others. Negative talk does little other than promote more depression.

- Make an effort to extend yourself to others. Teenagers who befriend other teenagers tend to be happier.

- Do what's expected of you. If you're not doing your best in school, try harder. If you refuse to help out around the house, change that. You'll feel better when you accomplish something.

- Practice random acts of kindness. Do something nice for someone for no reason at all.

- You'll feel good about yourself.

- Take care of your body. Eat the right amount of food. Get the right amount of rest.

- Exercise. Stay away from drugs and alcohol.

- Dress nicely. There really is something to the idea that when you look nice, you feel better about yourself. Of course, don't overdo it by getting obsessed with your looks or by dressing provocatively.

You can't force yourself to be happy when life has dumped on you. But you don't have to be a passive recipient of depression either. Depression is a condition you can fight. It doesn't have to be permanent. If you are not able to fight your way out of depression, talk to a parent or another adult about getting professional help.

Voices of Victory

You hear it all the time from teenagers who've been abused. They all say they hate God. I know. I've said it before, too. But someone told me that God cries every time I do. I can believe in a God who does that. I don't know why I was abused, but I don't want to believe that it means that the whole world and even God are bad, too. I really don't.

— Vicki, age 16

When Will Recovery Be Complete?

When you watch a movie, it is normal to ask how long the film lasts. Likewise, when school is out for the winter holidays or the summer break, you may count the days until your holiday is over and your life gets back to normal. We like to know in advance how long something will last so we can be ready for whatever comes next.

Some common questions trauma survivors ask about dealing with the pain of emotional or sexual abuse are . . .

- "When will it be over?"

- "How long until I feel normal?"

- "Will I always be depressed/angry/hurt/scared?"

It's normal to wonder about these things. No doubt you look forward to the day when all your troubles are behind you. There are no exact answers to these questions. A lot depends on how hard you work to understand yourself and your emotions. But we do know that those survivors who successfully recover from trauma have several things in common. Here are some major factors that determine when you will start feeling that recovery is working:

◇ **The severity of your trauma.** The number of traumatic events, the length of time you were exposed to abuse, and your reaction to the abuse play a role in recovery. For understandable reasons, the greater the abuse experience, the longer it takes to feel normal once again.

◇ **Your family situation—then and now.** If you have positive support from your family or other people you love, your chance of recovery is greatly improved. We all need loving people around us, especially following tough times.

◇ **Other problems you've acquired.** It's hard enough to get over abusive treatment, but if you have drug or alcohol problems, recovery is made tougher. Likewise, problems such as eating disorders, medical conditions, and legal troubles can keep you from focusing on treatment needs.

◇ **Your personal strengths and weaknesses.** Your personality may have more to do with your eventual success than any other factor. Teenagers who are optimistic (think positively), commit themselves to change, and trust those who want to help them are the most likely to feel better with the passage of time.

As hard as it may be, you will be doing yourself a favor to honestly look at your situation so that you can know exactly how much work there is to do. Make a commitment to take one small step forward every day. Before long, you'll be further down the road to recovery than you may have believed possible!

Talk About It

Take a quick inventory of your current situation:

How do you rate your trauma when you compare it to what "normal" people go through?

1 _____ 10
less   same   greater

How do you rate the support you have from the people around you—family, friends, helping professionals?

1 _____ 10
less   same   greater

How do rate your personal commitment to change?

1 _____ 10
weak   medium   strong

What are some of the biggest obstacles that keep you from recovering from your trauma?

1.

2.

3.

4.

In what way can you make better use of your family/friends or helping professionals to help you beat your current struggle?

1.

2.

3.

4.

Think About It! If you were abused, what happened to you was unusual in that it is not what should happen to a young person. You deserve better. Wouldn't it be wonderful to travel back in time and erase your abusive experience? As marvelous as that would be it's not possible. Sometimes children are hurt by people who are ill. And good people become victims of someone else's bad choices. That's not the way life is supposed to work. But because something bad happened to you does not mean you are a bad person, or that you deserved what you got, or that you should feel guilty. Time itself works to heal old wounds. Your commitment to work toward recovery helps speed the healing process. Your willingness to let others help you is a step in the right direction.

Useful Tip

Grief is not something that happens only after someone dies. You can grieve things like a lost childhood or a broken family. Help yourself through the grief process by writing your feelings in a journal or creating a life book with pictures and memories. Talk with a friend or adult who has gone through a grief experience similar to yours. Make a list of the negative and positive things that have happened because of your experience.

Believing Is Healing

The experience of sexual abuse hurts so badly that it can cause a victim to quit believing—in herself, in others, in life, in God, in goodness. In short, the pain of abuse can make a survivor feel suspicious about almost anything.

The ability to believe is an often overlooked part of recovery from trauma. But take note of those people who make it past their troublesome past. In general, they . . .

Believe that they are better than others seem to think

Believe that there is a God who can strengthen them

Believe that life moves forward, not backward

Believe that humankind—themselves included—is mostly good

Believe that change can and will occur

Young people who believe have a different vision than those who do not. Belief is not about "sight" as we commonly think of seeing. It is about looking at the world in a positive, but realistic, light. Take note that people can believe in the wrong things. For example:

Millions of Jewish people were killed in World War II because of misguided beliefs.

Untold numbers of young people abuse drugs or alcohol because of misguided beliefs.

Fortunes are wasted in senseless ways because of misguided beliefs.

Perpetrators abuse victims because of misguided beliefs.

People live lives of despair because of misguided beliefs.

Mistakes from the past are repeated because of misguided beliefs.

Beliefs can be good or they can be bad. Beliefs can motivate people to do good or to cause destruction. What you believe is important. Abuse survivors may be tempted to say, "I don't believe in anything or anyone." The truth is, we all believe in something. Recovery includes examining your beliefs. Knowing yourself and what you believe gives you a new way of knowing that life can be what you want it to be.

Dig Deep

Think hard. What is your response to each of the following belief statements?

"I believe that abuse survivors are likely to live a life of unhappiness."

"I believe that my problems will eventually fade away if I give it time."

"I believe that hard work can overcome mountains of problems."

"I believe that there is a God who looks out for people."

"I believe that bad things happen to people as punishment."

As you examine your responses to the above statements, what can you discover about yourself?

_____

_____

Reality check. Do you let others determine what and how you believe? Explain.

_____

_____

For each word listed below, think of a word that means the opposite:

Fear   _____

Hesitation   _____

Depression   _____

Suspicion   _____

Worry   _____

What do you want to believe that you currently struggle to believe?

_____

_____

Think About It!

Believing in yourself means acting as if you are "real." When you believe in yourself, you love yourself. To believe that you are lovable does not simply mean that you have a feeling for yourself. Self-love is not just a feeling. Self-love does not even mean that you always like yourself. Loving yourself means that you have faith in yourself. You believe that you can and will keep getting better. Believing in yourself means that you do what you can to make yourself a better person. And when you do that, you help others become better, too.

Voices of Victory

I'm going to be honest. I went for a long time without believing in anything. I was so wide open to what everyone else thought that I didn't know what's up. I tried everything hoping it would make me happy—drugs, sex. You name it, I tried it. Finally I got tired of chasing happiness. Once I just chilled and quit trying to be what I thought everyone wanted me to be, I started feeling better. I was me. I still don't know myself as well as I want to, but I'm getting there.

—Rachel, age 15

Give Yourself a Health Checkup

After your experience of sexual trauma, you have probably wondered, "How healthy am I?" Maybe you've even asked this question from the opposite direction: "How sick am I?" Trauma of any kind causes emotional wounds or sores, or breaks. Emotional pain is perhaps the most lasting harmful effect from sexual abuse. In the same way that physical injury can result in poor health, emotional injury can affect your mental health.

The term "mental health" can be hard to grasp. While experts give different definitions of how a normally healthy person act, thinks, and feels, it is a safe bet that you would be hard pressed to find a single person who is completely healthy from a mental standpoint. Despite this, we all wish to be as healthy as possible. The traumas and disappointments of life can get in the way, but every teenager is capable of making progress toward "normal" mental health.

Most mental health experts agree that normally healthy people . . .

★ Believe that they are equal to others in their worth

★ Trust their feelings and are not afraid to be themselves

★ Have a knack for judging situations correctly

★ Solve problems rather than create them

★ Enjoy friendships, but also feel comfortable when they're alone

★ Are able to build lasting relationships based on love and respect

★ Have a sense of humor that is not hostile or crude

★ Tolerate people who differ from them

★ Enjoy learning and look for ways to make themselves better

★ Show balanced emotions

The experience of sexual trauma can push a young person to feel and be anything but normal. The effect of abuse may leave you feeling fearful, unsure, bitter, intolerant, withdrawn, and confused. Life is not intended to be that way. Treatment involves changing abnormal characteristics, replacing them with thoughts, feelings, and behaviors that are more normal.

What's Your Perspective?

Tracy's Story

As a child, Tracy was mistreated in just about every way a girl could be mistreated. She was emotionally, physically, and sexually abused. Many of the adults in her world abused drugs or alcohol. She seldom heard loving remarks. Tracy had friends, but their kindness could not overcome all the negatives in her world. By the time she reached the teenage years, she felt anything but "normal" or "healthy."

Is Tracy a bad person simply because her life experiences were unkind?   Yes   No

Now that Tracy is older, what adjustments can she make in the way she thinks, feels, and acts?

_____

_____

_____

What obstacles keep Tracy from becoming a healthier person?

_____

_____

What have people said and done to you to make you feel emotionally unhealthy?

_____

_____

_____

As you read the list of "normal" characteristics on the previous page, which ones do you possess?

_____

_____

_____

Assignment

Think of someone you consider to be a normally healthy person. What traits does he/she have that you are lacking? Over the coming days and weeks, make an effort to be more like that person.

Think About It! We don't usually think of a "normal" person as being extraordinary. We don't call a normal person a hero. We don't say she is a superstar. We don't think of normal people as standing out in a crowd. After all, they're only, well, normal. Perhaps it's time to change what we think of as "normal." Normal people are balanced. Normal people get things done. Others lean on normal people for support. Hurting people want the advice of someone who is normal. There is something strangely attractive about these people. Maybe normal people *are* extraordinary. Maybe normal people *are* heroes. Maybe normal people *are* superstars. Maybe normal people *do* stand out in a crowd. Maybe we need to rethink the word "normal." Wouldn't you like to be one of them?

Behavior Watch: Being Perfectly Normal

Some people say that there is no such thing as a perfectly normal person. That's probably true since everyone has their own quirks and peculiar traits. The experience of sexual abuse can cause a teenager to wonder if she will ever be normal. The answer is *Yes, you can be just as normal as anyone else.* To determine if your thoughts, emotions, and behaviors are normal, regularly ask yourself these questions:

- Am I being real or am I trying to be something I am not?

- Do my choices help me become a better person?

- Do my choices help others become better people?

- Do I try too hard to hide my flaws?

- Are my emotions, behaviors, attitudes, or opinions way out of line in comparison to everyone else?

- Am I really happy or do I simply pretend?

Normal teenagers are able to make adjustments. Normal does not mean perfect. Normal simply means that you are genuinely trying to be the best you that's possible.

What's Next?

If you were given a crystal ball and could look into the future, chances are you would take a peek. How many times have you wondered if you will get married and, if so, what that person will be like? Or perhaps you wonder if someone who hurt you in the past will be punished for the harm he did to you. Or just maybe you hope that you can break the chain of emotional struggles that currently has you trapped. Most of us want to know what's next in life. Maybe you wonder . . .

- If life is going to get better

- How comfortable you will be in adulthood

- If you will be rich or poor

- What decisions you should make

- Whom you can count on to be a friend

- Whom to believe

- What precautions you should take

- How things will turn out

Let's face it. Life can be a scary thing. If the past has been unkind, what's to keep the future from being the same—or worse! As hard as it is to make sense of the past, it is even more difficult to understand the present. And the future? It's impossible to know what the future holds. More people worry about the future than any other thing. Being able to look ahead would give you a feeling of being in control. We all want a shining light to live by, some assurance that everything will be all right.

As odd as this may seem, being able to predict the future probably wouldn't be as great as it first seems. For one thing, it might make you cocky if you knew everything there is to know. Or maybe if you knew the future, you'd become lazy. Or who knows? You might take advantage of what you know and use it against your friends or family. In short, knowing what comes next might turn you into a monster of sorts!

There is one thing we do know about the future, and that is that the decisions you make today will go with you tomorrow. It's dangerous to plod from one day to the next without a purpose. You can't predict what will happen tomorrow, but by doing all you can to take care of yourself today, you are increasing the probability that the future will be bright.

Your Reflections

Daydream for a moment:

If I had lots of money, I would . . .

_____

_____

If I could, I would make sure that . . .

_____

_____

I'm going to be . . .

_____

_____

Something about the past I intend to change is . . .

_____

_____

Now let's do a reality check.

Things I can change about my family situation include:

_____

_____

_____

Things I can change about myself include:

_____

_____

_____

What is the best thing you can do to make your future better?

_____

_____

Think About It!

It's easy to worry about the future—too easy. It's harder to plan for the future. One of the lures of an abusive past is to dwell on what was rather than think about what can be. While it's healthy to look at the past and learn from your experiences, it's even healthier to look at where you are going, so that when you get there you will know what to do.

Useful Tip

Bright futures are not built with truckloads of money or mountains of popularity or tons of power. Bright futures are built on things you can't see or touch—things like a healthy self-esteem, a few close friendships, a strong education, and good social skills. Build your future on those things, and who knows—maybe you'll pick up a few extra perks along the way.

——Finding a Purpose——

Discouragement is common among sexual abuse survivors. You've been through good times and bad times, and too often it seems that the bad things outnumber the good. You've been told by well-meaning friends to "keep your chin up," but every time you lift up your chin, someone hits you, knocking you down to reality again. People who are close to you promise that they're going to see to it that life gets better—and then they let you down or someone else gets in their way. You promise yourself that you won't make the same mistakes you've always made, but when temptation comes, you give in. A young person can take only so much hurt and disappointment before giving up.

Every trauma survivor needs to feel that there is a purpose to her life. If there is no real reason for living . . .

Why keep trying to get better?

Why try to get along?

Why try to understand the past?

Why do what other people tell you?

Why not give up?

Here's a statement that seems simple, but is actually hard to understand: *It's not a teenager's situation or circumstances that drag her down. What defeats her is her belief that there's no purpose to life.* Trauma survivors who win at life say things like . . .

I want to help other teenagers who've been through the same thing I've been through.

In a strange way, I appreciate all the little things in life more than I used to.

All of my troubles make me more understanding of other kids who act the way I once did.

I intend to be a great parent to my own children.

I've figured out that I need to learn as much as I can right now so that I can be independent when I'm older.

When you become an adult and look back on your past, you may be forced to say, "Life wasn't easy on me when I was young." But the hard work you do right now may also allow you to say, "Life wasn't easy on me when I was young, but I'm a stronger person in spite of it!"

What Are Your Thoughts?

In what ways have you been discouraged by the things that have happened to you?

_____

_____

_____

_____

Complete the following sentences:

A dream that keeps me focused on my personal growth is . . .

_____

_____

Something I really hope will happen to me is . . .

_____

_____

When one of my friends seems to be feeling down I try to pick her up by . . .

_____

_____

Ways that I will be a better person because of my experiences include:

1.

2.

3.

4.

5.

Think About It! There's nothing more rewarding in life than finding your place in the world. Finding a purpose does not mean landing the perfect job or doing something to bring you fame and fortune. You find a purpose when you believe that you are someone special, that life is worth living, and that you can make a difference in someone else's life. Purpose comes to those who look beyond their flaws and weaknesses and see that the world needs something that they have.

Behavior Watch: Discouragement

Discouraged? Here are some signs to watch out for:

- No real interest in the things teenagers normally do

- When you imagine the future, it looks pretty bleak

- An "I don't care" attitude

- Depression that won't quit

Useful Tip

Sometimes teenagers try too hard to be happy. Next time you're around a group of teens take special note of the loudest member of the group. Chances are he's trying so hard to have a good time that he'll never get there. Happiness is best when it comes in small doses—going to a movie with a friend, helping someone out, going out to lunch. It's not necessary to party hard to find happiness.

Tracking Down Feelings

When you drive a new car, everything works like a charm. Turn the key and the engine roars. It's that simple. But as time passes, the engine does not run quite as smoothly as it did when it was brand-new. The car needs to be checked out, tuned up, even overhauled. Not that teenagers are as simple to understand as car engines (and that's no easy feat), but the two can be compared. At different stages of your life, it's a good habit to take an inventory of where your feelings come from. Like a car needs to be checked out for flaws, you can scan your emotions to discover what needs to be fine-tuned in your life. For example, a girl may scan her body and emotions and trace . . .

★ A weak self-esteem to comments made to her by controlling or critical adults

★ Feelings of fear to memories of being stalked by an abusive person

★ Difficulty trusting to being hurt after having been promised that it wouldn't happen again

★ A lack of personal confidence to people who said, "You're no good."

★ Depression to the experience of being left out by family or friends

★ Feelings of helplessness to being abused over and over

★ An "I don't care" attitude to one personal defeat after another

★ Sleep problems to the tension caused by being on edge when an abuser was around

Counselors frequently use the word "insight" to describe the breakthroughs that occur when a teenager learns something new about herself. Insight means you understand yourself. Insight means you understand other people. Insight means you have examined yourself and your world—and parts of your experience begin to make sense.

The best time to track down your feelings is after an event is over. No matter how badly you handled a situation, be open enough to ask yourself tough questions, such as . .

What happened to trigger me to act as I did?

How does my past influence the way I act in the present?

Am I making the same mistakes that I have made in the past?

Was I in control of myself, or did the situation control me?

Did the choices I made help me or hurt me?

What am I capable of being that will make me a better person?

Instead of kicking yourself for making mistakes, you can learn from them. Every layer of understanding that you peel back will reveal something new about you. The deeper you dig, the stronger you will become. Everyone makes mistakes. Everyone second-guesses the decisions they make. It's the teenagers who learn from the past who develop the greatest understanding of themselves.

It's Your Turn

What are some mistakes that you make regularly?

_____

_____

_____

_____

Pick one of the mistakes you named above. Think about some of the reasons you keep making that mistake.

_____

_____

_____

Answer True or False:

     T   F   I usually just act without thinking of *why* I do or say certain things.

     T   F   When people give me honest feedback about my behavior, I listen so I can learn.

     T   F   I think I can do a better job of understanding myself and others.

     T   F   When I experience a negative emotion, I'd rather not think about where it came from.

     T   F   When I learn something new about myself, it motivates me to know more.

I plan to learn from my experiences by doing the following:

_____

_____

_____

_____

Think About It! Many teenagers talk about how they were shaped by their experiences—some good, others not so good. It's true, you are who you are in large part because of what you've been through. But there's a difference between the teenager who simply suffers through an experience and the one who learns from it. The one who learns from life finds herself in control of where she will go next.

Useful Tip

Take time to be alone. Sit still for a few moments. Take a check of your body. What parts of your body are tense? Pay special attention to your face muscles. Are they tight? Try to relax your face. Check your stomach. Tense? Breathe easily and deeply. What about your hands and feet? Pretend that you can actually feel the blood flowing through them. When your body is at peace, your mind is much more effective.

Voices of Victory

Where am I now? To be honest, I'm not as far as I want to be. But I'm a heck of a lot farther along than I used to be. I know myself so much better now than I did a month, a year, five years ago. I was so lost. I'm finding myself now.

—Jodi, age 18

Being All You

Teenagers who are mad and argumentative all the time are no fun to be around. Even though their sour temperament may be related to a tragedy like sexual abuse, it's still unpleasant to hang around people who seem to be mad 24/7.

There's another kind of teenager who is difficult to be around—one you may not have thought to put in the same category as the defiant teen. Young people who never get angry, never say a cross word, never stand up to anyone, and never voice their real feelings become annoying after a period of time. These teens seem to have an internal computer program that forces them to be nice and sweet and sugary and polite all the time.

Maybe it's a bit of a stretch to say that the "always nice" teenager is as difficult to deal with as the "always mad" teen, but healthy teenagers find a comfort zone somewhere in the middle. When they feel negative, they express those emotions. When they feel positive, they express those emotions, too. They can be completely themselves.

Something happens to a teenager when she finds a way to be thoroughly real. "Real" teenagers . . .

- Experience less stress

- Discover things about themselves and make appropriate changes

- Find it easier to get along with teenagers who are like them and those who are not

- Experience lower highs and higher lows

- Keep from self-destructing

- Become well enough acquainted with themselves to get better

- Appreciate the little things other people do for them

- Are not too self-centered

- Express their opinions without coming across as opinionated

Being all of yourself means you can accept the good and the bad. Self-acceptance keeps you from being something you are not. Other people have a way of knowing who's real and who's not. Those who are the genuine article find it easier to overcome life's traumas.

Sound Off

Some emotions I tend to express too strongly include:

_____

_____

_____

_____

Some emotions I have a hard time expressing include:

_____

_____

_____

_____

One way I can tell if another teenager is well-rounded is . . .

_____

_____

One way I can tell if another teenager is *not* well-rounded is . . .

_____

_____

Some skills I'd like to develop to help me become a more well-rounded person include:

_____

_____

_____

_____

Think About It! As you work to become a better person, it's not necessary to be a different person. Better will do just fine. Teenagers who are real don't want to be someone else. They simply try to become aware of their shortcomings and work to improve on them.

Voices of Victory

When my mother's boyfriend started abusing me, he threatened me and made it sound like I'd be in trouble if anyone found out. Like a good little girl, I kept my mouth shut. For two years I didn't say a word. And then it slipped out. I told my aunt what was happening. She gave me permission to quit being so nice. She told me it was time to stand up for myself. That was the best advice I ever got.

—Amberlee, age 17

Behavior Watch: Dependence

All teenagers depend on other people to some degree. The saying that "No man is an island" is true. But you can go too far in the other direction by depending too much on one person. Teens who may be too dependent on others often have these traits:

- Feels uncomfortable without a boyfriend
- Puts up with more "crap" than is reasonable
- Hangs on to a relationship even after "the thrill is gone"
- Turns the other way if the boyfriend cheats on her
- Tolerates alcohol/drug abuse
- Too quick to give the other person a second (or third or fourth) chance

Give Yourself Permission

Sometimes it's hard to understand why you feel as you do. Many abuse survivors report that they experience strong feelings even when a situation doesn't necessarily call for a big emotional reaction. For example:

You see an adult who is correcting a child in public and it irritates you that adults have so much power over children. You know firsthand how humiliating it is to be embarrassed in front of others. A knot swells in your stomach and you wish you could tell that adult to mind his own business.

A really nice young man has been giving you lots of attention lately. On the one hand, you are flattered and want to take the relationship a step further. On the other hand, you are mad at yourself because you swore to yourself a long time ago that you were through with males because they all want the same thing from girls.

You're in a group of teenagers and someone makes a joke about girls who are "easy picking" for boys. That comment sets you off as you tell the jokester exactly what you think.

You cannot help but be influenced by your past. If you have been mistreated in any way, of course you will become upset if you see another person's rights being violated, especially a child's. If you have previously allowed yourself to be close to a male and then that male hurt you, you may resist that "falling in love again" feeling. Or if people make jokes about things that touch a sensitive nerve in you, your response may be strong.

It's not wrong for a teenager to feel whatever emotions she feels. Whether or not others would have handled the situation the same way you did is not really important. What is important is that you ask yourself meaningful questions about the causes and effects of your emotions. In other words, you must ask yourself questions like . . .

Am I feeling as I do because of my past experiences?

Does this situation bring back bad memories that I have not yet untangled?

Is my reaction helping me or hurting me?

What can I learn about others and myself from the way I feel right now?

Was I correct to react the way I did?

Give yourself permission to feel every emotion that surges through your body. But be smart. Learn why you think and feel as you do so that you can be completely *you*.

Having Your Say

What really sets you off? It may be a situation, a comment, or a queasy feeling in your stomach.

_____

_____

_____

_____

How is your reaction related to your past? What is it about those situations that drag up bad memories for you?

_____

_____

_____

_____

Is it right or wrong to feel the way you feel at those times? Explain.

_____

_____

_____

_____

Which emotions do you show too strongly? Not strongly enough?

Too Strongly	**Not Strongly Enough**
_____	_____
_____	_____
_____	_____

What can you learn about yourself as you observe the way you react to unpleasant situations?

_____

_____

_____

Finish this sentence: I will give myself permission to feel every emotion, but I can improve on the way I express myself by . . .

_____

_____

Assignment

Over the next few days, develop two lists. In the first list, write down the ways you expressed your emotions one year ago. In the second list, write down the ways you express your emotions right now. Look for improvements you've made. Also look for ways you can start to or continue to improve.

My Emotions—Last Year

_____

_____

_____

_____

My Emotions—Today

_____

_____

_____

_____

Think About It! Too often abuse survivors are told that they should not feel the way they feel. That's the wrong message. You cannot help but feel as you do. The right message should be: Let yourself feel all of your emotions. When you do, observe yourself. Ask yourself questions. Take every opportunity to learn more about who you are.

Voices of Victory

Some days I think I've made it. Other days I think I'm never going to get over the abuse. It's a fight. But that's what life is, isn't it? It's a fight. Fighters train to win. That's what I'm doing. I'm in training.

—Elle, age 17

═══════Now and Forever═══════

Even after the act of abuse is over, the abuse victim sometimes cannot help but bring the event into the present. The anger and hurt she feels do not go away quickly. Unwanted memories from the past make it seem that the abuse will go on forever. Sure, the past is the past. Everyone knows that. But the past can be dragged into the present when an abuse survivor says things like:

I wish I were dead!

I never want to be close to anyone again.

Nothing will ever be the same again.

Why is my life so much worse than everyone else's?

I'm mad and no one can ever make me feel happy.

I hate you! I hate everything about you!

Men just want one thing from me. That's all they ever think about.

It is completely natural to hate the bad things that have happened to you. Anger can be a curious friend that does not go away. The good news about anger is that the emotion you feel now does not have to last forever. Your "negative" emotions can be used to serve their purpose, but rather than drag them around forever, you can lay them to rest.

When anger and related emotions are limited to the present and then set aside until they are needed again, they don't have that damaging effect of lingering forever. Survivors get better when they . . .

1. Allow themselves to feel the emotion

2. Use the emotion in its intended way

3. Let go of the emotion until it is needed again

Statements like "I wish I were dead" or "I hate you" can be turned into something positive rather than something negative. Strong words such as these may express how you feel *right now*. They show that right now you want things to change. They can motivate you to change for the better *right now*.

The anger and hurt and shame and anxiety you feel because you were abused do not have to ruin you. They do not need to ruin your relationships. Believe it or not, these feelings may mean things like . . .

I love myself enough to stand up for my rights.

I love other people enough to respect their rights.

I refuse to let someone else hurt me, because I'm better than that.

I care about the future, so I'm going to try to make it as good as possible.

Forever is a long time. Abuse survivors learn the difference between words like "now" and "forever." Right now you may feel negative emotions. Those emotions can actually be useful. But when they have been appropriately used, they should be set aside until the next time they are needed.

It's Your Turn

What "negative" feelings do you experience over and over again?

_____

_____

_____

_____

_____

In what ways do you want to be better?

_____

_____

_____

_____

Look again at the list of emotions you just made. Which ones do you tend to use too much?

_____

_____

_____

_____

Finish this sentence:
I can help myself use my emotions positively by . . .

_____

_____

_____

_____

Think About It!

Many abuse survivors wonder how long the anger and hurt will last. The answer is, "These emotions will last as long as you use them." A teenager's feelings do not turn off and on automatically. In some ways, emotions are like a light switch. Flip the switch, and the light comes on. Flip it again, and it goes off. Trauma is a switch that turns on certain feelings. Those feelings can guide you to get out of darkness into the safety of the light. Once you get to where you need to be, the feelings that helped you get there should be turned off. Like a light bulb, overuse of emotions can eventually result in burnout.

Voices of Victory

My friends will tell you that I used to complain all the time that I wanted to die. I didn't want to die. If that's what I really wanted to do, I would have done it. What I really wanted was to get out of the hell I was living. One time when I said that I wanted to die, my friend shouted at me and told me to do something about it. I was stunned. I thought about what my friend said and realized she was right. I whined a lot about how bad my life was, but I was doing absolutely nothing to make it better. So instead of complaining that I wanted to die, I decided I should do a better job of living. That's what I did. You know what? I got what I wanted. The old angry part of me died and a new person came to life!

—Michelle, age 17

Some Other
New Harbinger Titles

Do-It-Yourself Eye Movement Technique for Emotional Healing, Item DIYE $13.95

Stop the Anger Now, Item SAGN $17.95

The Self-Esteem Workbook, Item SEWB $18.95

The Habit Change Workbook, Item HBCW $19.95

The Memory Workbook, Item MMWB $18.95

The Anxiety & Phobia Workbook, 3rd edition, Item PHO3 $19.95

Beyond Anxiety & Phobia, Item BYAP $19.95

The Self-Nourishment Companion, Item SNC $10.95

The Healing Sorrow Workbook, Item HSW $17.95

The Daily Relaxer, Item DALY $12.95

Stop Controlling Me!, Item SCM $13.95

Lift Your Mood Now, Item LYMN $12.95

An End to Panic, 2nd edition, Item END2 $19.95

Serenity to Go, Item STG $12.95

The Depression Workbook, Item DEP $19.95

The OCD Workbook, Item OCDWK $18.95

The Anger Control Workbook, Item ACWB $17.95

Flying without Fear, Item FLY $14.95

The Shyness & Social Anxiety Workbook, Item SHYW $16.95

The Relaxation & Stress Reduction Workbook, 5th edition, Item RS5 $19.95

Energy Tapping, Item ETAP $15.95

Stop Walking on Eggshells, Item WOE $15.95

Angry All the Time, Item ALL 13.95

Living without Procrastination, Item LWD $12.95

Hypnosis for Change, 3rd edition, Item HYP3 $16.95

Toxic Coworkers, Item TOXC $13.95

Letting Go of Anger, Item LET $13.95

Call **toll free, 1-800-748-6273,** or log on to our online bookstore at **www.newharbinger.com** to order. Have your Visa or Mastercard number ready. Or send a check for the titles you want to New Harbinger Publications, Inc., 5674 Shattuck Ave., Oakland, CA 94609. Include $4.50 for the first book and 75¢ for each additional book, to cover shipping and handling. (California residents please include appropriate sales tax.) Allow two to five weeks for delivery.

Prices subject to change without notice.